Hiking
Waterfalls
Ohio

A Guide to the State's Best Waterfall Hikes

Mary Reed

FALCONGUIDES

ESSEX, CONNECTICUT

For all Ohio conservationists, past, present, and future, who work
to preserve these wild areas for future generations

FALCONGUIDES®

An imprint of Globe Pequot, the trade division of The Rowman & Littlefield Publishing Group, Inc.
4501 Forbes Blvd., Ste. 200
Lanham, MD 20706
www.rowman.com

Falcon and FalconGuides are registered trademarks and Make Adventure Your Story is a trademark of The
Rowman & Littlefield Publishing Group, Inc.

Distributed by NATIONAL BOOK NETWORK

Copyright © 2024 The Rowman & Littlefield Publishing Group, Inc.

Photos by Mary Reed unless otherwise noted

Maps by The Rowman & Littlefield Publishing Group, Inc.

British Library Cataloguing-in-Publication Information available

Library of Congress Cataloging-in-Publication Data
ISBN 978-1-4930-7246-0 (paper: alk. paper)
ISBN 978-1-4930-7247-7 (electronic)

♾™ The paper used in this publication meets the minimum requirements of American National Standard
for Information Sciences—Permanence of Paper for Printed Library Materials, ANSI / NISO Z39.48-1992.

The author and The Rowman & Littlefield Publishing Group, Inc., assume no liability
for accidents happening to, or injuries sustained by, readers who engage in the
activities described in this book.

Contents

The Hikes

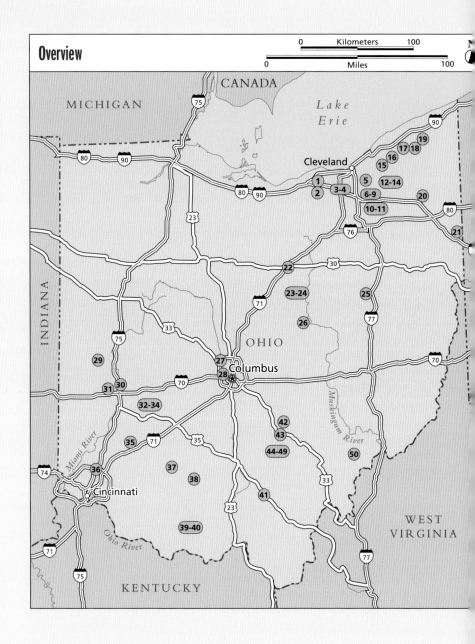

Overview

0 Kilometers 100

0 Miles 100

MICHIGAN

CANADA

Lake Erie

Cleveland

OHIO

Columbus

INDIANA

WEST VIRGINIA

KENTUCKY

Miami River

Muskingum River

Ohio River

Cincinnati

Acknowledgments

Thank you to the land managers, naturalists, and marketing professionals who provided ideas, answered questions, and reviewed information on the waterfalls in this book. There are too many to name, but you know who you are and you have my gratitude. Thank you to the Davis family for being my Cleveland base: Sabrina, Ryan, and Kat. Thanks to other friends who helped hike, drive, schlep, and sometimes model for me: Valerie Hura, Lisa Daris, Marcia Goldstein, Chelsea Hindenach, Michelle Greenfield, Mike Dombroski, and Hylie and Bruce Voss. Thank you to Terry Eiler for feedback on photographing waterfalls. As always, a final thank you to my partner, Attila Horvath, who serves as muse, model, chauffeur, first reader, and number-one supporter.

Introduction

Waterfalls are a full-sensory experience. They're beautiful, making them easy on the eyes and relatively easy to photograph. They tend to be surrounded by beautiful landscapes. The sound of waterfalls—often heard before seen—can be everything from soothing to exhilarating. You can feel the wind and spray coming off large falls and, where allowed, you can interact with them by wading and splashing. There's often a distinct smell that goes along with the moist landscape created by waterfalls. You may not want to take the chance of tasting water from them, though!

Why an entire book dedicated to hiking to waterfalls in Ohio? Well, why not? While most hiking books may need to consider variety in location, length, and features, a hiking waterfalls book can concentrate on getting you directly to the best waterfall hikes in the state. That's exactly what this project is all about.

While the state of Ohio is largely framed by water—Lake Erie, the Ohio River—it is not known for its waterfalls. That's understandable, as there is not a great deal of land in the state with the geologic plus hydrologic conditions to create waterfalls. Yet the Buckeye State has dozens of falls, and a handful of genuinely spectacular ones.

Hikes in this book were selected based on waterfalls, of course, but also length and quality of the hikes. There are some big, beautiful, and famous falls in Ohio that you can't hike to. Think Cuyahoga Falls or Chagrin Falls. Other falls out there may have no proper trail to them, may be on private property, or may be too ephemeral to expect to see a waterfall when you go.

For each hike in this book, expect a short to medium-length hike to a waterfall that should be there when you arrive, unless it's late summer or fall and it hasn't rained lately. Each chapter includes an easy-to-read map, a descriptive photograph, at-a-glance information about the destination, and point-by-point hiking directions.

How Are Waterfalls Created?

When water crosses the land in the form of a stream or a river, it encounters rock with varying levels of hardness or resistance. That is, some rock is more easily eroded by water than other rock. For example, limestone is a much softer rock than sandstone. Therefore, where sandstone and limestone meet abruptly along a streambed, you'll often find waterfalls.

This is the same process that makes some waterfalls "migrate" upstream. Take Cedar Falls in the Edge of Appalachia Preserve System (hike 40) in southwest Ohio, for example. The rock at the top, or lip, of the falls is sandstone. The softer limestone has worn away below. As the limestone continues to erode, the sandstone sticks out farther and farther above the limestone. After the substrate can no longer support the top level of sandstone, it will collapse. The waterfall is now farther upstream than before, and you can see large chunks of sandstone lying in the creek after detaching and falling.

Blue Hen Falls

Definitions

What is a waterfall? This may seem like a silly question; surely you know it when you see it. But different people have different ideas as to when fast-moving water that is increasingly vertical becomes an actual waterfall. That said, here are some guidelines for how to understand what kind of waterfall to expect as you read this book.

Block: A plunging waterfall that extends across the width of a river or stream. See West Falls (hike 2) for an example.

Shelf: A very short waterfall, up to 3 feet tall, that extends across the width of a river or stream. See Hell Hollow Waterfalls (hike 18).

Cascade: A cascade tumbles down a craggy rock face or a series of rock levels. This type of waterfall can be as horizontal as vertical, or even more so. See Bridal Veil Falls (hike 8) as an example.

Chute: A pressurized flow of water shooting out of a narrow passage. Some sections of Clifton Gorge are narrow enough that the water charges through a chute (hike 33).

Tiered: The water from a stream or creek falls over multiple drops. See Fallsville Falls for an example (hike 37).

Plunge: A waterfall that drops vertically and loses contact with the rock face. Dundee Falls is a good example of this (hike 25).

Cave: Rock shelters, or recess caves, are common in southeast Ohio's Hocking Hills. In this case, a waterfall plunges over the lip of the cave, sometimes allowing you to hike behind the waterfall. Whispering Cave Falls (hike 47) and Ash Cave Falls (hike 49) are good examples.

Ephemeral: A waterfall that is only present during certain times of the year, mainly when there is plentiful late-winter or spring rain. These falls are usually so low as to be practically nonexistent in the summer and fall. This is noted in each chapter where applicable.

How to Use This Guide

Hiking Waterfalls Ohio is designed to be highly visual and quickly referenced. Start by selecting a region: Northeast Ohio, Central Ohio, Southwest Ohio, or Southeast Ohio. (There are no natural waterfalls in northwest Ohio.) Each region begins with a section intro, where you're given a sweeping look at the lay of the land. Following each section intro are the hikes within that region. Each hike chapter begins with a short summary. You'll learn what to expect from the hike, the waterfall, and what sets it apart from other waterfalls in the book. If your interest is piqued, read on. If not, skip to the next hike. The hike specifications are fairly self-explanatory.

Height of falls: How tall and, if applicable, how wide or long the falls are.

Type of falls: See list above for descriptions.

Distance: This is the length of the hike, as well as if it is a loop or an out-and-back.

Difficulty: This is how difficult the hike is. If the hike is harder than easy, a brief explanation is included.

Hiking time: Approximate amount of time it will take you to complete the hike.

Trail name(s): The name of the trail or trails that take you to the waterfall(s).

Trail surface: What to expect in terms of whether the trail is dirt—the most common—or if it is gravel, paved, on a boardwalk, etc.

Seasons and hours: The best time to visit the falls, plus the hours of operation for the destination.

Canine compatibility: This lets you know right away if dogs are allowed. Leashed dogs are permitted at most—but not all—of these destinations.

Trailhead facilities: This helps you plan ahead by knowing if you can count on finding facilities like water, restrooms, picnic areas, etc., at the trailhead. Know that when water is available, it is often seasonal.

Trail contact: The name, phone number, and website address for the entity that manages each site.

Special considerations: If there is anything else to know ahead of time, look for it here. It may include any fees (atypical in Ohio), hunting seasons, and so on.

Finding the trailhead: Dependable directions from a major intersection or a nearby town or city right down to where you'll want to park.

The Hike is the meat of the chapter. Detailed and honest, it's the author's carefully researched impression of the trail. While it's impossible to cover everything, you can rest assured that you won't miss what's important.

Miles and Directions provides comprehensive, point-by-point mileage cues to identify all turns and trail name changes, as well as points of interest.

Hike Information

This section contains information to help you with planning, especially if you are traveling and spending the night at or near your destination.

Local information. This is the contact info for the local visitors bureau. This is a good place to start if you want to learn more about what events happen nearby, where to eat, lodging, and so on. Additionally, if there is a nature center or visitor center on-site, contact info is provided here.

Organizations. If there is a friends group, volunteer organization, or other supporting organization for the park, park system, or preserve, contact information is listed here.

Hiking groups. The largest and most active local hiking clubs or groups are listed in this section. But this is by no means an exhaustive list. Do a Google search or a search on meetup.com to find even more hiking groups. Or consider a Google search that further refines what you're looking for in a hiking group. For example, you can search for an affinity hiking group based on things like gender, race/ethnicity, or LGBTQ+ friendliness.

Camping. If there is on-site or adjacent camping, contact and reservation info is included here.

Slip this guide into your backpack and begin your adventure. Enjoy your time in the outdoors—and remember to pack out what you pack in.

Leave No Trace

As the saying goes, take nothing but pictures, leave nothing but footprints, kill nothing but time. Here's a refresher on Leave No Trace principles.

- Before heading out, plan your trip and be prepared. This not only includes becoming familiar with the route you will be traveling but also knowing the park's or forest's rules and regulations, what type of weather can be expected, and where you can find help in case of emergencies. And speaking of emergencies, you should avoid hiking alone, but if you do, always let someone know your hike plans—your route and what time you expect to complete your hike.

- Be sure to dispose of waste properly. Remember the rule: Pack it in, pack it out. Whatever trash you make on your hike, pack it out with you for proper disposal.

- Of course, when you're on the trail and you gotta go, you gotta go. And despite what some might say, dog droppings are not good fertilizer. For human waste, dig a 6- to 8-inch cat hole well off the trail and away from water sources (about 200 feet) to deposit the waste, then cover the hole. If you're on a hike with your dog, carry poop bags and pack the waste out. In sensitive areas, a WAG bag is increasingly common for human waste as well.

- Leave what you find! Leave any historic artifacts (like arrowheads), antlers, rocks, or wildflowers you may find. Don't deface rocks or plants.
- Be respectful of wildlife. Never feed animals, and only view them from a distance. If you bring your dog, be sure to keep it under control and avoid encounters.
- Finally, be considerate of others. Be respectful while on the trail—talk quietly, take breaks off the trail, yield to other trail users, and make sure to manage your pet.

© Leave No Trace: www.LNT.org

For more information and helpful tips, visit Leave No Trace online at lnt.org.

An additional ethic to consider in this era of social media is to tag responsibly. This means you should not go off-trail and get that "perfect shot" that will encourage others to go off-trail as well. Do not go to a permit-only preserve and then drop a pin with GPS coordinates. In other words, use your social media to reinforce, rather than disobey, Leave No Trace principles.

The 10 Essentials

American Hiking Society recommends you pack the "10 Essentials" every time you head out for a hike. Whether you plan to be gone for a couple of hours or several months, make sure to pack these items. Become familiar with these items and know how to use them.

1. Appropriate Footwear
   Happy feet make for pleasant hiking. Think about traction, support, and protection when selecting well-fitting shoes or boots.

2. Navigation
   While phones and GPS units are handy, they aren't always reliable in the backcountry; consider carrying a paper map and compass as a backup, and know how to use them.

3. Water (and a way to purify it)
   As a guideline, plan for half a liter of water per hour in moderate temperatures/terrain. Carry enough water for your trip, and know where and how to treat water while you're out on the trail.

4. Food
   Pack calorie-dense foods to help fuel your hike, and carry an extra portion in case you are out longer than expected.

5. Rain Gear & Dry-Fast Layers
   The weather forecast is not always right. Dress in layers to adjust to changing weather and activity levels. Wear moisture-wicking cloths and carry a warm hat.

6. Safety Items (light, fire, and a whistle)
   Have means to start an emergency fire, signal for help, and see the trail and your map in the dark.

7. First-Aid Kit

Supplies to treat illness or injury are only as helpful as your knowledge of how to use them. Take a class to gain the skills needed to administer first aid and CPR.

8. Knife or Multi-Tool

With countless uses, a multi-tool can help with gear repair and first aid.

9. Sun Protection

Sunscreen, sunglasses, and sun-protective clothing should be used in every season regardless of temperature or cloud cover.

10. Shelter

Protection from the elements is necessary in the event you are injured or stranded. A lightweight, inexpensive space blanket is a great option.

The 11th Essential

The 10 Essentials have been around for a long time. So have modern humans in the woods, with our prepackaged food, toiletries, and more things that can quickly become litter. Sometimes a piece of trash is accidentally dropped or left behind. Other times, inconsiderate users purposefully do not pack out what they packed in. Marrying Leave No Trace and the 10 Essentials, there is an 11th Essential to add to the list: a trash bag. Stuff a small bag into your own day pack and pick up trash along the way. If everyone adopts this 11th Essential and picks up trash—even to a small degree—the cumulative effect can be profound.

Waterfall Safety

Hiking presents its own inherent hazards—weather conditions, injury, beestings, falling trees. When you come prepared and stay aware, these hazards can be minimized and you can enjoy a fun and safe day of hiking. Some hazards are specific to waterfall hikes, however.

Stream crossings. Several hikes in this book involve stream crossings. This can be part of the fun, for sure. But be prepared. Bring water shoes or plan to cross barefoot. A hiking pole is a great tool to have to help you maintain your balance when crossing a stream with flowing water. That said, when the water is too high, swift, and/or cold, it can be simply too dangerous to cross. Exercise good judgment and be prepared to turn around when necessary.

Flash floods. By definition, hiking to a waterfall means you will generally be hiking near a river or stream. Waterfalls have higher volume and are more attractive with a lot of water, meaning that right after a rain is a great time to visit. That said, flash floods are exactly what the terms says—water can rise extremely fast, creating dangerous and even deadly conditions. Exercise caution.

How to Photograph Waterfalls

When to Go

Most waterfalls in Ohio do not enjoy particularly high flow; even those that are spring fed or lie below a dam can dry up to a trickle in summer and fall. Late winter to early spring is the best season to photograph Ohio waterfalls. When you can capture that combination of rain and melting snow, you can find extraordinarily high volumes of water, completely transforming an otherwise modestly flowing waterfall into a thundering cataract. Photographing right after rain is a good time as well, because everything will be wet and you won't have sharp contrast between, say, wet rock and dry rock surrounding the falls.

Because you want even light (without high contrast between sun and shade) for photographing waterfalls, choose to go early in the morning or late in the evening, when the illumination of the scene is even and light displays the color cast of sunrise or sunset. Otherwise, you want to shoot when there is cloud cover keeping the light even. While a blue-sky day and light shining directly on a waterfall can be a delight to the human eye, it seldom turns out well in a photograph.

Tools

If you want to get the highest quality photograph, you'll need to invest in good camera gear. Start with a digital SLR (single-lens reflex) or mirrorless camera. A good camera will allow you full control over settings (see below). A tripod is necessary for taking long-exposure photos: Most exposures longer than 1/15 of a second will not be sharp if you are holding the camera by hand. You will likely need a circular polarizing filter or a neutral density (ND) filter to assist in controlling the light. You can hand turn a polarizing filter on your lens to decrease (or increase) reflections. The polarizing filter will reduce the exposure an f-stop or two, decreasing the amount of light entering your camera through the lens. A neutral density filter is like a pair of sunglasses for your camera. ND filters reduce the exposure by the number of stops indicated on the filter. The higher the number on the ND filter, the less light it will allow in.

Settings

To make a long exposure you need to control the balance between exposure (f-stop) and camera light sensitivity (ISO). If you'd like to get a nice, silky waterfall photo, you'll need a shutter speed of ½ to 1 second to get some water movement without too much "noise" or surrounding blur in the photo, like blurry leaves if there is any breeze at all. Generally, in cloudy or low-light conditions, you can achieve a shutter speed of ½ second or slower by setting a low ISO (try 100) and a high f-stop (try f-22). You can usually adjust these settings in most of your camera modes, whether manual, shutter priority, or aperture priority. If there is something of interest that can be created by a really long exposure, like swirling water, an exposure of 5 or 10 seconds can bring striking results. This would generally require a neutral density filter on top of the settings described above. To capture the unusual hues of light at pre-dawn,

Lower Falls at Conkles Hollow, more commonly known as Conkles Hollow Falls

sunrise, sunset, and dusk you will need to select a light balance other than auto white balance. The white balance setting of daylight will allow the capture of the extreme hues of sunrise and sunset.

Composition

Waterfalls are easy to compose; it's practically impossible to go wrong. One option is to make a full-frame photo where the waterfall takes up pretty much the entirety of the frame, whether it's the original 3:4 ratio or after the photo has been cropped. You have possibly heard about the rule of thirds in photography, where a main subject might take up one-third of the frame, allowing the rest of the frame to display the surrounding layers of landscape or composition. The rule of thirds can be useful for a waterfall that plunges and then continues to flow rapidly along the stream below. Another composition tool that can apply to waterfall photography is using a strong foreground. It may be a swirl of water, stones with water crashing over them, wildflowers, and so on. This layered composition tool will allow you to build a foreground, middle ground, and background to your photograph.

iPhone Photos

If you want a beautiful, silky waterfall shot for social media, and don't necessarily want to make a print, the most recent iPhone models can make that happen. Make sure your iPhone is set to "Live" mode. When you take your photo of the waterfall in "Live" mode, steady your iPhone. You might try to use an existing wall, rock, tree, or a monopod to keep your iPhone still when you press the shutter. Alternatively, stand with your feet shoulder-width apart, one foot slightly in front of the other and your elbows pressed into your body. Once you've taken the photo, pull it up for review. At that point, you can click on the live menu and select "long exposure" to get an Instagram-worthy silky waterfall photograph.

Public and Private Lands in Ohio

Should you become a waterfall enthusiast, know that there are more waterfalls in Ohio than are listed in this book. If you decide to go looking for them, a good handle on what is legal on what type of land is helpful. Wherever you go, it is always imperative to practice Leave No Trace principles.

Private land. Private land that is open to the public includes parcels owned by private nature preserves. For example, Cedar Falls (hike 40) is on property owned by The Nature Conservancy, Quiverheart Falls (hike 39) is owned by the Arc of Appalachia preserve system, and Hemlock Falls (hike 23) is made accessible by the efforts of the North Central Ohio Land Conservancy. Private landowners have their own rules and regulations. You can usually find these listed on their websites or by calling ahead. Expect to see restrictions as to where and when you can hike, usually only on-trail and during daylight hours. Look for special events hosted by the preserve managers, which may allow for the occasional off-trail hike to special features. Often dogs are not permitted, so plan ahead to know when to leave your best friend at home.

Metro parks and county parks. Parks owned by cities and counties tend to serve large population bases. Because of heavy use, expect wide trails and rules plus infrastructure to keep you on them. Be sensitive to overuse, and follow rules and regulations that help protect these areas for future generations. These parks are often family friendly, with nature centers and naturalist programs. Leashed dogs are generally permitted, and hunting is restricted or altogether banned. Both Cleveland Metroparks and Lake Metroparks have several reservations with waterfalls. (See the Northeast Ohio section.)

State parks. Ohio residents and visitors are lucky to have state parks around the entire Buckeye State (ohiodnr.gov/discover-and-learn/safety-conservation/about-odnr/division-parks-watercraft/state-parks-boating), and entrance is free of charge—the vast majority of US states charge for access to state parks. Ohio state parks are open to everyone for day use generally from 6 a.m. to 11 p.m. Many state parks have campgrounds and visitor centers. Generally, off-trail hiking is not allowed and leashed dogs are allowed. These rules are extremely important in popular state parks like Hocking Hills State Park (hikes 46–49), which is known for its waterfalls. If you hike from Upper Falls to Lower Falls (hike 46) you won't see the spring wildflowers that are abundant in other parts of the park. This is due to heavy use as well as poor use—that is, off-trail hiking and unleashed dogs. In order to keep Ohio state parks free to enter, consider supporting the Ohio State Parks Foundation (ohiostateparksfoundation.org).

A cascade along Mill Creek in Hogback Ridge Park

State nature preserves. The Ohio Department of Natural Resources Division of Natural Areas and Preserves (ohiodnr.gov/discover-and-learn/safety-conservation/about-odnr/nature-preserves/nature-preserves) exists to protect and preserve special places for future generations. Because the preserves primarily protect species located on-site—rather than for recreation—know that it is a privilege to be able to hike at DNAP preserves. Conkles Hollow (hike 44) is a good example of a state nature preserve, as well as an example of how difficult it can be to get the public to follow Leave No Trace principles. It is imperative to follow the rules, which state that you must stay on trails at all times, and you must leave your pet at home. There are quite a few permit-only preserves where trails do not exist (therefore off-trail hiking is a must). Contact the division to get a free permit to visit these preserves. Some of them, like Boch Hollow State Nature Preserve, are home to beautiful waterfalls.

State forests. Ohio state forests operate under looser regulations than Ohio state parks. Off-trail hiking is generally allowed, as are other activities, such as horseback riding, mountain biking, hunting, and so on. Leashed dogs are also permitted. When you visit a state forest like Hocking State Forest to see Big Spring Hollow Falls (hike 45) you can explore to find other waterfalls—ephemeral falls in the spring are common. You should have confident navigation skills if you plan to hike off-trail, and you should always have a safety plan in place. This means avoid hiking alone and always tell someone of your plans and when you expect to return home. State forests are also home to logging and oil and gas development. Make sure the area you plan to visit isn't temporarily closed for one of these uses. Finally, familiarize yourself with hunting seasons, especially rifle seasons. It's best to avoid these properties altogether during deer rifle season, and wearing hunter orange is a good idea.

State wildlife management areas. Wildlife management areas are places set aside for hunting, trapping, and fishing. Leashed dogs are permitted. Dundee Falls (hike 25) and Fallsville Falls (hike 37) both are located in state WMAs. In general, there are no official trails at all in wildlife management areas, so off-trail hiking is allowed. In both waterfalls on WMA lands listed in this book, there are trails to the falls; they exist somewhere between social trails and official trails. It is best to avoid wildlife management areas during any firearm hunting seasons. It's also a good idea to wear hunter orange when you hike on these properties.

National forests. Ohio's only national forest, the Wayne National Forest, also has looser regulations than city, county, and state parks. For example, off-trail hiking and dogs are permitted. There are no waterfall hikes featured in this book within the Wayne National Forest. If you decide to hike off-trail in search of waterfalls, exercise the same caution you would in a state forest: You should have confident navigation skills and should always have a safety plan in place. This means avoid hiking alone, and always tell someone of your plans and when you expect to return home. As with state forests, the Wayne is host to logging and mining plus gas development. It's best to avoid the Wayne during deer rifle season, and wearing hunter orange is a good idea. As of 2024, the U.S. Forest Service proposed to change the name of the Wayne National Forest to Buckeye National Forest, in response to requests from Native American tribes and others.

National parks. Ohio's only national park, Cuyahoga Valley National Park is home to some of the most popular waterfalls in the state, like Brandywine Falls (hike 11) and Blue Hen Falls (hike 10). Leashed dogs are permitted in the park. Outside of frontcountry, high-trafficked areas, it is legal to hike off-trail in Cuyahoga Valley National Park, and online you will find information on off-trail waterfalls. Again, it is imperative to have excellent navigation skills and a safety plan in place before you hike off-trail. Go to a visitor center and talk to a ranger before attempting cross-country hiking. Tell someone where you are going and when you plan to return. ***Note:*** Drones are not permitted in the national park.

Hemlock Trees

In Ohio, anywhere you come across plunging or cascading water, you are generally in a shady, wet valley where you will find yourself among stately, evergreen hemlock trees (*Tsuga canadensis*). Many hikes in this book make note of the hemlock trees surrounding the waterfalls. Native to Ohio, hemlocks are easily identified by their short, flat needles and small cones. Unfortunately, hemlock trees are under a major threat. The aphid-like pest known as the hemlock woolly adelgid is an insect that feeds on the sap of the trees, eventually killing them. Woolly adelgids are easy to identify; they

Cedar Falls, Hocking Hill State Park

look like little white cotton balls or white mold collected at the base of the needles where the needles meet bark. Different land management agencies have different treatment plans. Learn more information, including what you can do and how to report sightings of hemlock woolly adelgid, at ohiodnr.gov/hwa.

There are other threats to hemlocks as well, primarily in the form of diseases caused by fungi. If and when you see hemlock trees in distress, go to the website above and report what you see. You can download the Great Lakes Early Detection Network (GLEDN) app at the Apple Store or from Google Play.

Buckeye Trail

Several hikes in this book invite you to "follow the blue blazes" to a beautiful water-fall. When you see the signature 2 x 6-inch Sherwin-Williams #2408 Sweeping Blue blaze, you know you are on the Buckeye Trail. The BT is a roughly 1,444-mile loop that makes its way around the entire Buckeye State. There are two formal termini: One is in northeast Ohio at Headlands Beach State Park; the other is in southwest Ohio in Cincinnati's Eden Park. Northeast Ohio is also home to the Little Loop, a 250-mile loop segment of the BT. Ultimately, it is a circular trail with no designated place to begin or end. But one great place to start is to follow the blue blazes to Linda Falls (hike 7), Bridal Veil Falls (hike 8), Blue Hen Falls (hike 10), and to the waterfalls along the BT/Grandma Gatewood Trail—Upper and Lower Falls (hike 46), Cedar Falls (hike 48), and Ash Cave Falls (hike 49). This section of the BT is also named for Emma "Grandma" Gatewood, the first woman to solo thru-hike the Appalachian Trail in 1955, at age 67. She was also a founding member of the Buckeye Trail Association, which was formed in 1959. Learn more at buckeyetrail.org.

A waterfall along the West Branch of the Rocky River

Map Resources

The maps in this book are easily referenced for the featured hikes. Begin at the trailhead, marked with the hike number. The featured trail is highlighted in yellow, and directional arrows tell you which way to hike, corresponding to the point-by-point directions. Additional info, like parking, water, and restroom availability, is easily seen on each map.

There are other map resources that can help you either find the trailhead, find other nearby trails, or get more detailed information should you want it. As far as finding the trailhead, you can plug in GPS directions or street addresses into Google Maps to find the trailhead (GPS coordinates are included in each "Finding the trailhead" entry in this book). Google Maps does show a few select trails as well.

If you are in a place that has no cell or wireless service (there are places like this in rural Ohio), you may already own a copy of the *DeLorme: Ohio Atlas & Gazetteer*. This resource can be helpful in finding your way around on local roads if you lose a signal. Should you attempt a backcountry trail in the Wayne National Forest or Shawnee State Forest, a USGS topo map is handy.

The Ohio Department of Natural Resources and some metro parks have their own map apps, available in the app store for iPhone or Android. The ODNR Detour web and mobile app has searchable digital map files for all ODNR properties. Each entry highlights a trail by name and gives the length and a short description of the trail.

The Cleveland Metroparks app has trail maps and recognizes your current location, much like the AllTrails app or Gaia GPS. Dayton's Five Rivers MetroParks and the Miami County Park District use the OuterSpatial app for digital mapping. These are also available in the app stores.

Trail Finder

Best Hikes for Multiple Waterfalls

3. Olmsted Falls
12. Sulphur Springs Falls
13. Double Decker and Quarry Rock Falls
16. Stoney Brook Falls
18. Hell Hollow Waterfalls
19. Mill Creek Falls, Hogback Ridge Park
20. Cascade and Minnehaha Falls
22. Fleming Falls
24. Big and Little Lyons Falls
25. Dundee Falls
27. Indian Run Falls
31. Oaks, Patty, and Martindale Falls
32. The Cascades
36. Sharon Woods Waterfalls
46. Upper and Lower Falls, Hocking Hills State Park
47. Whispering Cave Falls

Best Waterfall Hikes for Water Access

12. Sulphur Springs Falls
18. Hell Hollow Waterfalls
19. Mill Creek Falls, Hogback Ridge Park
25. Dundee Falls
28. Millikin Falls
37. Fallsville Falls
C. Girdled Road Reservation Waterfall

Note: While crossing the creeks and wading may be allowed, swimming is prohibited.

Best Wheelchair-Accessible Waterfall Views

4. Berea Falls
11. Brandywine Falls (upper overlook)
15. Buttermilk Falls
26. Honey Run Waterfall
28. Millikin Falls
29. Greenville Falls
34. Cedar Cliff Falls
36. Sharon Woods Waterfalls
49. Ash Cave Falls
D. Blackhand Gorge Waterfalls (Blackhand Trail)

Tallest Waterfalls

5. Mill Creek Falls, Garfield Park Reservation
11. Brandywine Falls
24. Big Lyons Falls
30. Charleston Falls
33. Amphitheater Falls
45. Big Spring Hollow Falls
47. Whispering Cave Falls
49. Ash Cave Falls

Best Year-Round Waterfall Hikes

2. West Falls
3. Olmsted Falls
4. Berea Falls
9. Great Falls of Tinker's Creek
10. Blue Hen Falls
11. Brandywine Falls
13. Double Decker and Quarry Rock Falls
21. Lanterman's Falls
28. Millikin Falls
46. Upper and Lower Falls, Hocking Hills State Park

Best High-Volume Waterfalls in Spring

2. West Falls
4. Berea Falls
5. Mill Creek Falls, Garfield Park Reservation
9. Great Falls of Tinker's Creek
11. Brandywine Falls
13. Double Decker and Quarry Rock Falls
25. Dundee Falls
28. Millikin Falls
29. Greenville Falls

Short Waterfall Hikes with Additional Mileage Options

1. Day's Dam Falls
6. Chippewa Creek Falls
7. Linda Falls
11. Brandywine Falls
16. Stoney Brook Falls
19. Mill Creek Falls, Hogback Ridge Park
21. Lanterman's Falls
23. Hemlock Falls
30. Charleston Falls
33. Amphitheater Falls
35. Horseshoe Falls
45. Big Spring Hollow Falls
46. Upper and Lower Falls, Hocking Hills State Park
48. Cedar Falls, Hocking Hills State Park
49. Ash Cave Falls
A. Mudcatcher Falls
B. Euclid Creek Waterfalls

Easiest Waterfall Hikes

1. Day's Dam Falls
3. Olmsted Falls
9. Great Falls of Tinker's Creek
27. Indian Run Falls
29. Greenville Falls
36. Sharon Woods Waterfalls
44. Lower Falls, Conkles Hollow State Nature Preserve (Gorge Trail)
49. Ash Cave Falls
50. Falls Run Falls

Best Waterfall Hikes for Seclusion

7. Linda Falls
25. Dundee Falls
38. Miller Falls
40. Cedar Falls, Edge of Appalachia Preserve
42. Rock Stalls Waterfall
50. Falls Run Falls
E. Ophir Falls

Waterfalls in the city of Olmsted Falls

Best Waterfall Hikes with Kids

Map Legend

Municipal
- ═(71)═ Interstate Highway
- ═(33)═ US Highway
- ═(87)═ State Road
- ═══ Local Road
- = = = = Gravel Road
- ├──┼──┤ Railroad
- ·····–··· State Boundary

Trails
- − − − − − Featured Trail
- - - - - - Trail
- ──── Paved Trail

Water Features
- Body of Water
- River/Creek
- Intermittent Stream
- Waterfall
- Spring

Symbols
- Bench
- Bridge
- Boardwalk
- ■ Building/Point of Interest
- ∩ Cave
- Inn/Lodging
- **P** Parking
- ▲ Peak/Elevation
- Picnic Area
- Restroom
- Scenic View/Overlook
- ‖‖‖‖‖ Steps
- ○ Town
- (1) Trailhead
- Visitor/Information Center
- Water

Land Management
- National Park/Forest
- Park/Preserve/Reservation

Mill Creek Falls in Garfield Park Reservation

Northeast Ohio

One of a few regions in Ohio with a relatively high concentration of waterfalls, northeast Ohio's falls are also close to the state's largest population base. Add in a wide variety of falls—plunges, cascades, tall, wide—and northeast Ohio is a great go-to for waterfalling. Most rivers and creeks in far northeast Ohio drain into Lake Erie, including most of those featured in this book, like the Rocky River, Brandywine Creek, Paine Creek, and Euclid Creek. Most of these streams and rivers that are Erie tributaries have the classic high shale bluffs. But there's no shortage of sandstone here, so you'll find that wide variety of falls.

Cleveland Metroparks and Lake Metroparks are both home to a number of waterfalls in northeast Ohio. These park systems have done a great job of providing access to the waterfalls via established trails, and they have plenty of other infrastructure, like nature centers and regular programming. Some even have camping or cabin options for overnight stays.

Cuyahoga Valley National Park is home to dozens of waterfalls. This book includes the beautiful and popular waterfalls that are accessible by established trails. Hiking off-trail is allowed in the park, which is open 24/7/365, so you can spend time looking for those falls. But only do so if you are a capable and experienced hiker who can properly employ Leave No Trace principles. Cuyahoga Valley National Park could easily keep you busy for an entire vacation, or an entire lifetime for that matter. In addition to the trailside and off-trail waterfalls, there are more than 125 miles of trails in the park. Additionally, signature features of the park include the Cuyahoga Valley Scenic Railroad and its Hike Aboard program, which lets you use the railroad as a shuttle for a small per-person fee (it runs seasonally; check the schedule and stops at cvsr.org/hike-aboard). The Ohio & Erie Canal Towpath Trail is more than 90 miles in length (20 miles are within Cuyahoga Valley National Park boundaries) and is open to hikers and cyclists alike. Embedded within the park is Blossom Music Center, summer home to the Cleveland Orchestra and a Live Nation concert venue.

As you visit waterfalls in northeast Ohio and the greater Cleveland area, you'll encounter names like Mill Creek, indicating that many of these waterways were once

Berea Falls

used to power early industry by way of water mills. The remnants of this early industry are still visible with dams, foundations, bridges, and more. You'll see that industry still thrives in this "rust belt" region.

Finally, take note of Lake Metroparks' Hell Hollow Wilderness Area, Hogback Ridge Park, and Girdled Road Reservation. Wading, creeking, and generally exploring the water is allowed at these sites, so enjoy!

1 Day's Dam Falls

Day's Dam Falls, also known as the 36th Street Ditch Falls, is where you'd least expect it—the waterfall isn't on a creek or river at all. The waterfall is the result of a storm drainage that pours over a shale cliff into the Black River valley. From the view below, you'd never know this. Whatever the origins, these falls are a pleasure to visit when the water is running high. As long as you're in the area, combine this outing with another to nearby East and West Falls.

Height of falls: About 25 feet
Type of falls: Plunge
Distance: 1.4-mile lollipop
Difficulty: Easy
Hiking time: About 40 minutes
Trail names: Bridgeway Trail, Waterfall Trail
Trail surface: Asphalt, dirt, wood chips

Seasons and hours: Best late winter to early spring; open daily, 8 a.m. to sunset
Canine compatibility: Leashed dogs permitted
Trailhead facilities: Restrooms, water, picnic area
Trail contact: Lorain County Metro Parks Black River Reservation; (440) 458-5121; lorain countymetroparks.com/black-river-reservation

Finding the trailhead: From I-90 exit 151 in Avon (west of Cleveland), take SR 611 west 2.9 miles to East River Road. Turn left (south) and go 1.1 miles to East 31st Street. Turn right (west) and go 0.4 mile to the park entrance on the left. The trailhead is on the south side of the lot, near the restrooms. GPS: N41 26.29' / W82 06.20'

The Hike

Close to East Falls and West Falls on the Black River, Day's Dam Falls is relatively unknown. Hike to this waterfall—quite substantial with enough water flow—on the popular, paved Bridgeway Trail to the unpaved Waterfall Trail loop. Most people who visit this park to get their workout bypass the Waterfall Trail; they shouldn't, because it's a worthwhile side trip. Start from the Day's Dam parking area with full amenities and take the Bridgeway Trail, which more or less parallels the Black River.

Descend gently into the Black River valley and hop on the Waterfall Trail, a short (0.5-mile) loop that takes you past the namesake falls. Also known as the 36th Street Ditch Falls or simply Ditch Falls, they do not have an official name. This location was used as a trash dump prior to the park system's taking it over in 1994.

Like most falls in Ohio, these are much more impressive in the spring or after a rain. While the falls look perfectly natural, they are the result of stormwater that's routed to this spot. They fall over a roughly 25-foot shale bluff, entering the Black River valley. Wear appropriate footwear—when the waterfall is flowing strongly after a rain, the trail can be muddy. Look for bluebells in the valley in spring.

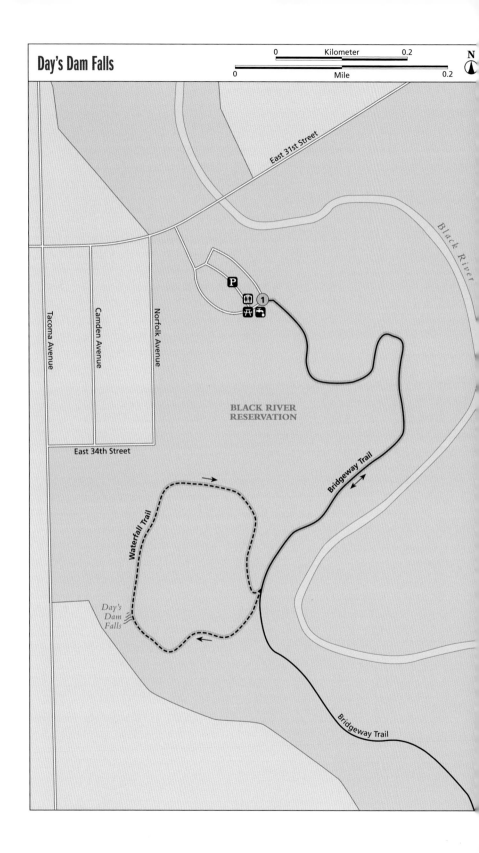

Day's Dam Falls

0   Kilometer   0.2

0   Mile   0.2

N

East 31st Street

Black River

P

1

Tacoma Avenue

Camden Avenue

Norfolk Avenue

BLACK RIVER
RESERVATION

East 34th Street

Bridgeway Trail

Waterfall Trail

Day's
Dam
Falls

Bridgeway Trail

Day's Dam Falls

Miles and Directions

0.0 Start at the trailhead on the south side of the parking lot at the trailhead kiosk. Walk along the asphalt trail.

0.5 Come to a junction where the signed Waterfall Trail begins on the right. Exit the asphalt and start the trail to complete it in a clockwise direction.

0.6 Arrive at the benches where you can view Day's Dam Falls to the left, through the woods.

0.9 Complete the Waterfall Trail loop. Turn left and walk onto the asphalt, retracing your steps to the trailhead.

1.4 Arrive back at the trailhead.

Hike Information

Local information: Lorain County Visitors Bureau; (440) 406-3119; loraincountyohio.gov/cvb

Organizations: The Friends of Metro Parks in Lorain County, Inc.; (440) 458-5121; loraincountymetroparks.com/volunteer

Hiking groups: Cleveland Hiking Club; clevelandhikingclub.org

Northeast Ohio Hiking Club; meetup.com/NEOHiking/

2 West Falls

The name Cascade Park says it all. Known locally for its two substantial cascades, West Falls and East Falls, Cascade Park and its waterfalls are not famous statewide, but they should be. If you're in northeast Ohio, it's well worth a visit to this little park with easy access to these thunderous falls. A nice trail to West Falls winds between the Black River and sandstone ledges.

Height of falls: 35 feet tall, up to 80 feet wide
Type of falls: Block
Distance: 0.9-mile loop with a spur to the waterfall
Difficulty: Moderate due to uneven terrain and stairs
Hiking time: About 30 minutes
Trail names: Ledges Loop, Bear's Den Connector
Trail surface: Asphalt, dirt, boardwalk

Seasons and hours: Best in spring; open daily, 8 a.m. to sunset
Canine compatibility: Dogs permitted on a 6-foot leash
Trailhead facilities: Water, restrooms, picnic area
Trail contact: Lorain County Metro Parks Cascade Park; (440) 458-5121; loraincounty metroparks.com/cascade-park

Finding the trailhead: From SR 57 in Elyria, turn south onto West River Road North and go 0.3 mile to Furnace Street. Take a left onto Furnace Street and then another immediate left onto Cascade Street. Drive down the hill to the parking area near the playground and picnic shelter. From here, cross the road and pick up the asphalt Riverside Trail. Take a right and walk to a set of steps that lead down to a trail with wood chips. This is where the Ledges Loop begins. GPS: N41 22.30' / W82 06.33'

The Hike

West Falls in Cascade Park is part of an urban oasis in many ways. The falls plunge beneath a highway bridge. But other than that bridge, you can feel far from the city on the hike to West Falls on the Ledges Loop, returning on the Bear's Den Connector. This is a family-friendly destination, especially when you combine the short hike with a stop at the playground, nature center (open only for programming; check the website), or a wintertime outing on the wide sledding hill.

Much of the trail parallels the Black River, which flows north into Lake Erie. The trail itself is sometimes pinched between the river and Berea Sandstone ledges more than 20 feet high. Look closely and you will see remnants of an old sandstone quarry here. This creates a cool location where species like the evergreen hemlock tree can thrive. Along the riparian corridor, you'll be hiking under sycamore and cottonwood trees. As you continue hiking toward the falls, you'll walk in the upstream direction

West Falls in Cascade Park

and follow the West Branch of the Black River, hence the name West Falls. Return on the Bear's Den Connector, which will take you past sandstone recess caves, suitable to protect animals and humans alike from rain and snow.

Indeed, this was home to Native Americans of the Erie and other tribes for millennia before European settlers moved in. The Lorain County Metro Parks arrowhead logo is a nod to this. Early excavations revealed arrowheads and other Native artifacts. In more recent history, Elyria is named for Heman Ely, who settled this area in the early 1800s and built a gristmill. In 1894 the Ely family deeded the land, now Cascade Park, to the city.

While you're here, be sure to stop by East Falls, which, at 30 feet high and 50 feet wide, is just as impressive as West Falls. East Falls is on the East Branch of the Black River, located in a separate section of the park, off Kerstetter Way. There is a parking lot and viewing platform for East Falls, but no trail. The city of Elyria installed LED lights to light up East Falls at night, and there is a live feed of the falls, searchable on YouTube.

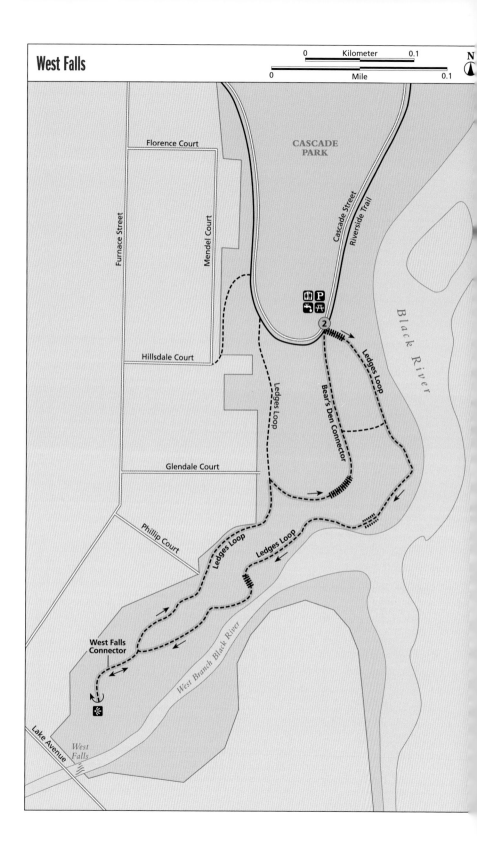

West Falls

CASCADE PARK

Florence Court

Furnace Street

Mendel Court

Hillsdale Court

Glendale Court

Phillip Court

Ledges Loop

Ledges Loop

Bear's Den Connector

Cascade Street

Riverside Trail

Black River

Ledges Loop

Ledges Loop

West Falls Connector

West Branch Black River

Lake Avenue

West Falls

Kilometer

Mile

N

Miles and Directions

0.0 From the asphalt Riverside Trail at the stairs with a rail, walk down the stairs to pick up the Ledges Loop trail and follow it as it parallels the river. In less than 500 feet, the trail enters the forest with cliffs and boulders, ascending stone steps. Continue until the trail eventually becomes paved.

0.4 The paved trail arrives at the end of a former pedestrian/bike bridge that crosses the river but is closed indefinitely. Take a left here and follow the dirt path to the waterfall overlook platform. After viewing the falls, return from the platform to this spot.

0.5 Returning to the paved trail by the closed pedestrian/bike bridge, take a left.

0.6 Come to a dirt trail on the right. This is the Bear's Den Connector. Take this trail to a set of wooden stairs. Take the stairs and descend to the bottom of the cliff.

0.8 Follow the trail straight, passing a footbridge on the right.

0.9 Arrive back at the trailhead.

Hike Information

Local information: Lorain County Visitors Bureau; (440) 406-3119; loraincountyohio .gov/cvb

Organizations: The Friends of Metro Parks in Lorain County, Inc.; (440) 458-5121; loraincountymetroparks.com/volunteer

Hiking groups: Cleveland Hiking Club; clevelandhikingclub.org

Northeast Ohio Hiking Club; meetup.com/NEOHiking/

3 Olmsted Falls

Most people know Olmsted Falls as the name of a town, and that it is. But the town's namesake is the waterfall itself. Hike this city park to Olmsted Falls and then to more waterfalls at the confluence of Plum Creek and the West Branch of the Rocky River. Between the sizable and varied falls plus old quarry remnants, it's a little gem well worth visiting even if the trail mileage is short.

Height of falls: Varies; most are a few feet high.
Type of falls: Cascade, plunge, shelf
Distance: 0.9 mile out and back
Difficulty: Easy
Hiking time: About 30 minutes
Trail names: Dan Waugh Nature Trail, unnamed trails
Trail surface: Gravel, dirt, pavement

Seasons and hours: Best in spring; open daily, sunrise to sunset
Canine compatibility: Leashed dogs permitted
Trailhead facilities: None; restrooms and water are available at East River Park.
Trail contact: David Fortier River Park and East River Park, City of Olmsted Falls; (440) 235-5550; olmstedfalls.org/residents/parks.php

Finding the trailhead: From I-480 in North Olmsted, take exit 6 and go south on SR 252 for 2.3 miles to Main Street. Turn left and go a few hundred feet. You'll see street parking and a parking lot on the left. GPS: N41 22.38' / W81 54.06'

The Hike

This is surely the highest waterfall-to-acreage park in the state. Begin in the heart of this little town in David Fortier River Park. Take the Dan Waugh Nature Trail to Olmsted Falls. Historical records show that Dan Waugh was a local man who wrote a weekly newspaper column titled "Nature Rambles" for the *Berea Sun*, beginning in 1948.

Olmsted Falls is both the name of the waterfall and the name of the town. The township had several names over the years, including Plum Creek Township, but eventually the township name was settled as Olmsted Township for the Olmsted family, who donated a library in return for the naming.

The hike continues downstream, paralleling Plum Creek. Pass the Charles A. Harding Memorial Bridge, a quaint covered bridge that spans the creek. It's named for an Olmsted Falls native who died in the World War II Battle of Normandy.

Then arrive at David Fortier River Park, named for an Olmsted Falls high school teacher and mayor who died in a car accident in 1986. This is where the real waterfall action is. At the confluence of Plum Creek and the West Branch of the Rocky River, you'll see waterfalls on both waterways. The waterfalls on Plum Creek end with large swirls of water before joining the West Branch of the Rocky River. On the West

Waterfalls near the confluence of Plum Creek and the West Fork of the Rocky River

Olmsted Falls

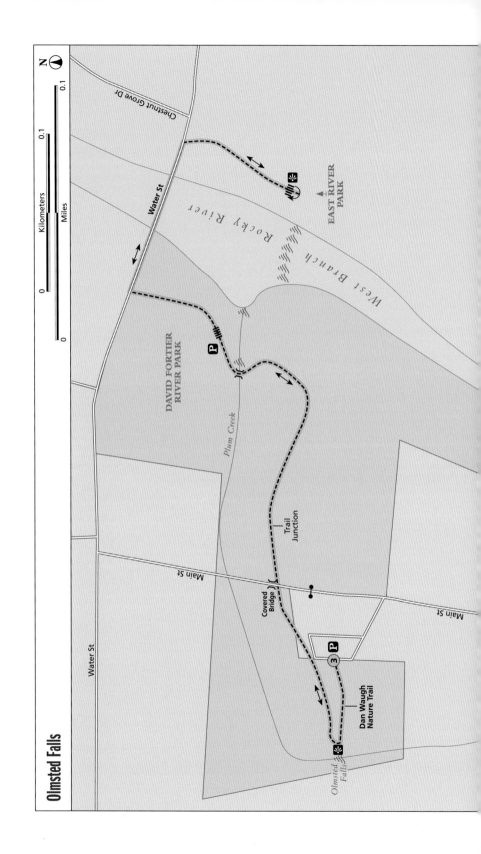

N

Kilometers
0   0.1   0.1

Miles
0   0.1

Chestnut Grove Dr

Water St

EAST RIVER PARK

West Branch Rocky River

DAVID FORTIER RIVER PARK

Plum Creek

Water St

Main St

Trail Junction

Covered Bridge

Main St

P

3

Dan Waugh Nature Trail

Olmsted Falls

Branch of the Rocky River, there are still more falls, including a shelf waterfall that spans the entire width of the river. This is a great picnic spot. There are plenty of places to unpack your lunch, from the rocks along the river to an old stone pavilion. Swimming is prohibited.

Speaking of stone, this area was once home to a sandstone quarry. You will see old millstones around the park, and the section of park north of Plum Creek is where the old quarry was. Today, a forest has grown back, and this little river valley is a pleasant and popular local gathering spot. In addition to the quarry, local history includes industry. Like pretty much all substantial waterfalls in Ohio, this area was once home to mills, in this case a sawmill and then a gristmill.

From David Fortier River Park, walk to Water Street and cross over the river. After crossing on the sidewalk, turn right and walk on a trail again. From the bridge you can get a great view of the confluence. On the other side of the river, now in East River Park, hike to an overlook platform where you get another great view of the confluence and the waterfalls. East River Park has restrooms and water.

Miles and Directions

0.0 Start at the Dan Waugh Nature Trail sign; walk into the woods and then to an overlook for Olmsted Falls. From here, continue hiking downstream.

0.1 Pass the covered bridge on your left and walk under an overpass. Come to a junction with another access path and turn left, continuing to parallel the creek.

0.2 Cross the creek on a footbridge and come to a parking lot. Walk to the road and take the sidewalk over the river.

0.3 After crossing the road bridge, turn right to enter Olmsted Falls East River Park. Walk the trail that parallels the West Branch of the Rocky River.

0.45 Take wooden steps up to an overlook platform. From here, turn around and retrace your steps to the trailhead.

0.9 Arrive back at the trailhead.

Hike Information

Local information: Destination Cleveland; (216) 875-6680; thisiscleveland.com
Organizations: Rocky River Nature Center (Cleveland Metroparks); (440) 734-6660; clevelandmetroparks.com/parks/visit/parks/rocky-river-reservation/rocky-river -nature-center; open daily, 9:30 a.m. to 5 p.m., except New Year's Day, Easter, Thanksgiving, Christmas Eve, and Christmas Day
Hiking groups: Cleveland Hiking Club; clevelandhikingclub.org
Northeast Ohio Hiking Club; meetup.com/NEOHiking/

4 Berea Falls

When you look at Berea Falls, you can see history. First, the geologic history. Harder Berea Sandstone and softer shale meet to create the falls themselves. Above the falls are rail lines that are still in use today, a representation of the region's industrial past and present. And then there's the history of Cleveland Metroparks. The first land purchased by the metroparks was in the Rocky River watershed, in 1919. Come create your own personal history by hiking to Berea Falls once or over and over again.

Height of falls: 25 feet
Type of falls: Tiered
Distance: 2.6 miles out and back
Difficulty: Easy
Hiking time: About 1 hour
Trail name: Bridle Trail
Trail surface: Crushed gravel
Seasons and hours: Good year-round; open daily, 6 a.m. to 11 p.m.
Canine compatibility: Leashed dogs permitted
Trailhead facilities: Vault toilet, picnic area

Trail contact: Cleveland Metroparks Rocky River Reservation; (440) 734-6660; clevelandmetroparks.com/parks/visit/parks/rocky-river-reservation
Rocky River Nature Center; (440) 734-6660; clevelandmetroparks.com/parks/visit/parks/rocky-river-reservation/rocky-river-nature-center
Special considerations: This is both a hiking trail and a bridle trail. All trail users should exercise courtesy and caution. Horses have right-of-way.

Finding the trailhead: From I-71 in Middleburg Heights, take exit 235 and go west on Bagley Road for 2.1 miles to Barrett Road. Turn right onto Barrett Road and go about 300 feet to Valley Parkway. Turn right onto Valley Parkway and go 1.1 miles to the Willow Bend Picnic Area on the right. From the picnic area, cross Valley Parkway to access the trail.
GPS: N41 23.25' / W81 52.11'

The Hike

The Rocky River Reservation is a park heavily used by Cleveland west siders. It's a worthwhile park to visit as a destination as well. Berea Falls has several tiers that plunge into pools. The backdrop is made up of arching stone railroad bridges. When flow is high, these falls are huge and quite impressive.

A start at Willow Bend Picnic Area makes for a nice day hike to the falls and back. (**Note:** Willow Bend parking may be full when the shelter is reserved, or inaccessible in very high water.) You will follow the well-constructed bridle trail between here and the falls. The trail closely parallels the Rocky River, with its high shale bluffs. The flow is generally reliable, in part due to the fact that water from regional stormwater sewers and treated water from sanitary sewers contribute to the flow. The key word is "treated": Water quality is good enough to support a population of stocked steelhead trout. Look for fly fishers late fall through early spring.

ea Falls

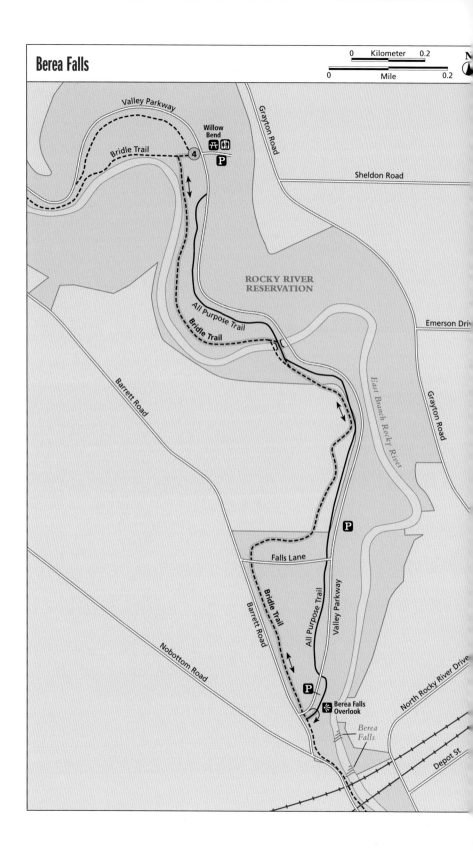

Berea Falls

Valley Parkway

Grayton Road

Sheldon Road

Willow Bend

P

Bridle Trail

ROCKY RIVER
RESERVATION

All Purpose Trail

Bridle Trail

Emerson Drive

Barrett Road

East Branch Rocky River

Grayton Road

P

Falls Lane

Bridle Trail

Barrett Road

All Purpose Trail

Valley Parkway

Nobottom Road

North Rocky River Drive

P

Berea Falls
Overlook

Berea
Falls

Depot St

Springtime brings many wildflowers, including skunk cabbage, phlox, and mayapple. Riparian tree species include maple, beech, buckeye, birch, and sycamore. Plenty of invasive plants have taken hold here too, like Japanese honeysuckle and autumn olive. Listen for the songs of cardinals and chickadees. Wildlife thrives here; don't be surprised if you see a white-tailed deer or even a coyote.

As you approach the falls, you may hear them before you see them. An overlook platform off the All Purpose Trail gives you an overview of the long, many-tiered waterfall. The Berea Sandstone was quarried around here and used for millstones and buildings in the 1800s. Both the sandstone and the town Berea were named by Christian settlers after a biblical locale.

While you're here, check out the Rocky River Nature Center (check online for programming) and other trails, including the Fort Hill Loop Trail, which takes you up the Fort Hill Stairs. From the top, you can view earthen walls built by Early Woodland people more than 2,000 years ago. You also get an expansive view of the Rocky River.

Miles and Directions

0.0 From the Willow Bend Picnic Area parking lot, cross Valley Parkway and take the All Purpose Trail away from the road for about 20 feet to a dirt path on the left. Follow the dirt path about 100 feet to a junction with the Bridle Trail, marked with a bridle trail blaze. Turn left.

0.5 The trail forks. The right fork is where horses cross the river. Take the left fork and walk up to the All Purpose Trail. Turn right to take the pedestrian bridge over the Rocky River. After crossing the river, turn right again to rejoin the Bridle Trail.

1.0 Cross Falls Lane.

1.3 Cross Valley Parkway and then turn left onto the All Purpose Trail. Walk the All Purpose Trail to the Berea Falls Overlook platform. From here, turn around and retrace your steps. (**Option:** You can return on the All Purpose Trail.)

2.6 Arrive back at the trailhead.

Hike Information

Local information: Destination Cleveland; (216) 875-6680; thisiscleveland.com
Hiking groups: Cleveland Hiking Club; clevelandhikingclub.org
Northeast Ohio Hiking Club; meetup.com/NEOHiking/

5 Mill Creek Falls, Garfield Park Reservation

As hard as it is to believe, the cascading Mill Creek Falls you look at today are 300 feet from the original falls—they were moved by hand in 1905. As the name implies, Mill Creek Falls originally housed milling operations but today serves as a place for recreation and respite in urban Cleveland. This is the tallest waterfall in Cuyahoga County and is just 6 miles from downtown Cleveland.

Height of falls: 48 feet
Type of falls: Cascade
Distance: 3.0 miles out and back
Difficulty: Easy
Hiking time: About 1 hour
Trail name: All Purpose Trail
Trail surface: Asphalt

Seasons and hours: Best late winter to early spring; open daily, 6 a.m. to 11 p.m.
Canine compatibility: Leashed dogs permitted
Trailhead facilities: Restrooms, picnic area
Trail contact: Cleveland Metroparks Garfield Park Reservation; (216) 206-1000; cleveland metroparks.com/parks/visit/parks/garfield -park-reservation

Finding the trailhead: From I-77 exit 159A south of Cleveland, take Harvard Road east 1.5 miles to Broadway Avenue. Turn right (south) and go 1.5 miles to the Garfield Park entrance on the right. Turn into the park and go straight 0.2 mile to a fork. Take the left fork to a stop sign. From the stop sign, the Trolley Turn Picnic Area parking is almost directly across the street. Pull into the parking lot and start at the trail kiosk on the All Purpose Trail, between the parking lot and the road. GPS: N41 25.47' / W81 36.37'

The Hike

The hike to Mill Creek Falls—on a paved path through an exceedingly narrow greenway—isn't an attraction in and of itself. But the payoff is Cuyahoga County's tallest waterfall, a beautiful 48-foot-tall cascade with an interesting history. If you're here just for the waterfall, there is a parking lot right above the falls off Webb Terrace. But put on your hiking shoes and you can get a 3.0-mile out-and-back workout in addition to viewing the falls.

In 1799 the first gristmill was built at the foot of Mill Creek Falls but was later moved to the top of the falls. Flour and lumber were milled for what was then Newburg Village. In 1857 the Cleveland steel industry got its start north of Mill Creek Falls when the Cleveland Rolling Mills opened. The north part of Newburg Township, including Mill Creek Falls, was annexed by Cleveland in 1873. But then the story gets more interesting. In 1905 the falls were moved—by hand, using picks and shovels—300 feet upstream to make room for the new route of the Cleveland and Pittsburgh Railroad.

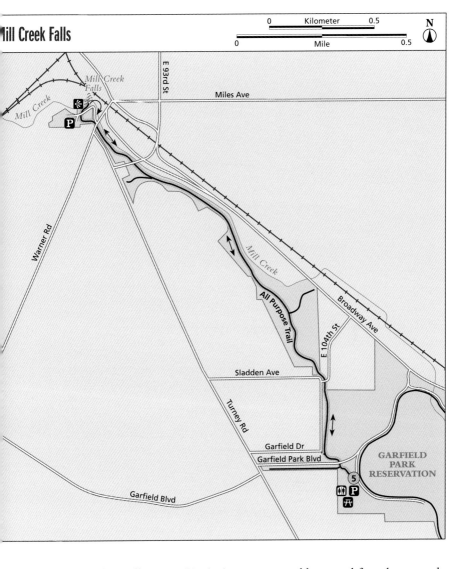

Beginning at the Trolley Turn Picnic Area—presumably named for where a trolley/streetcar turned around—it's a straight shot to the falls. This is an urban outing, so you will see a lot of backyards. It's perfect if you're just a "backyard birder"; common species like sparrows abound here, in addition to harder to identify but easy to appreciate birds like warblers. You'll also walk through some wooded areas and get occasional views of Mill Creek.

The trail ends at a viewing platform for Mill Creek Falls, with an upper and lower deck. After viewing the falls up close, you can walk a few hundred feet downstream to get another view of the falls, but this view can be obscured by leaves. Late fall to early spring will get you a clear view of the falls from here.

Mill Creek Falls in the Garfield Park Reservation

Miles and Directions

0.0 Begin at the trail kiosk on the All Purpose Trail by the Trolley Turn Picnic Area parking area and head northwest. In about 300 feet, turn right and cross Garfield Park Boulevard.

0.3 Cross Sladden Avenue/East 104th Street.

0.6 The trail forks; take the left fork.

1.2 The trail forks again; take the right fork.

1.4 Cross Warner Road.

1.5 Arrive at the parking lot for Mill Creek Falls. Cross the driveway and take the boardwalk/ sidewalk to the falls overlook. Retrace your steps to the trailhead.

3.0 Arrive back at the trailhead.

Hike Information

Local information: Destination Cleveland; (216) 875-6680; thisiscleveland.com
Hiking groups: Cleveland Hiking Club; clevelandhikingclub.org
Northeast Ohio Hiking Club; meetup.com/NEOHiking/

6 Chippewa Creek Falls

The main waterfall along Chippewa Creek, right below the stone bridge over SR 82, is easy to hear but hard to see when there are leaves on the trees. But downstream, the creek continues to run, drop, and pool among the large boulders. A trail takes you right down to the creek in this section along a hike that parallels the creek its entire length. This is an all-around great hike for water lovers.

Height of falls: 10 feet
Type of falls: Plunge
Distance: 2.8 miles out and back
Difficulty: Easy
Hiking time: About 1 hour
Trail names: Hemlock Trail, Gorge Loop
Trail surface: Dirt
Seasons and hours: Best late fall through early spring; open daily, 6 a.m. to 11 p.m.
Canine compatibility: Leashed dogs permitted
Trailhead facilities: Picnic area only; restrooms available at the nature center

Trail contact: Cleveland Metroparks Brecksville Reservation; (440) 526-1012; clevelandmetroparks.com/parks/visit/parks/brecksville-reservation
Brecksville Nature Center; (440) 526-1012; clevelandmetroparks.com/parks/visit/parks/brecksville-reservation/brecksville-nature-center; open daily, 9:30 a.m. to 5 p.m., except New Year's Day, Easter, Thanksgiving, Christmas Eve, and Christmas Day

Finding the trailhead: From I-77 in Brecksville, take exit 149 and go east on SR 82 for 1.3 miles to Chippewa Creek Drive. Turn right and go 1.3 miles to the Lower Chippewa Creek Picnic Area. Cross Chippewa Creek Drive to pick up the Hemlock Trail trailhead. GPS: N41 18.58' / W81 36.03'

The Hike

The "Emerald Necklace" of Cleveland Metroparks is proof that you can fit a lot of high-quality hiking in narrow spaces. Case in point is the Brecksville Reservation, which is the largest property in the park system. Here the Hemlock Trail squeezes in between the road and the All Purpose Trail on one side and Chippewa Creek on the other. It provides everything you want in an urban getaway: a wooded hike along a rushing creek, complete with a side trail that takes you to the edge of the water. Chippewa Creek Gorge, cut by Chippewa Creek, was created after the last glacier retreated about 12,000 years ago. Chippewa is the Anglicized word for the Ojibwe people.

Starting from the Chippewa Creek Picnic Area, cross the park road and pick up the trail at a trailhead sign. The trail blaze is a white silhouette of an evergreen tree on a green background, and you will see the namesake hemlock trees in the cool Chippewa Creek Gorge. You'll also see other evergreens, like scotch and Austrian pine. Spring is a great time to hike this trail. Not only are water levels higher, but wildflowers include jack-in-the-pulpit, wild geranium, waterleaf, and bloodroot.

Hikers enjoy waterfalls downstream of Chippewa Creek Falls

Chippewa Creek Falls

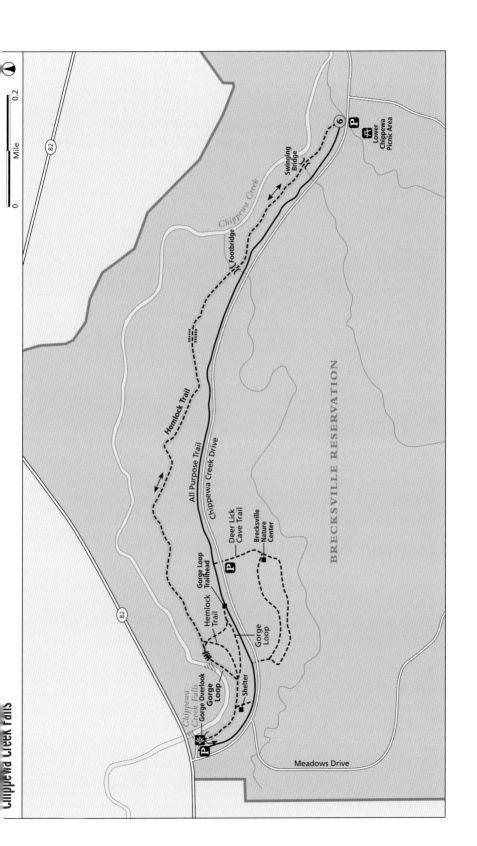

0 Mile 0.2

82

Chippewa Creek

Hemlock Trail

All Purpose Trail

Chippewa Creek Drive

Deer Lick
Cave Trail

Brecksville
Nature Center

P

Gorge Loop
Trailhead

Hemlock
Trail

Gorge
Loop

Footbridge

Swinging
Bridge

6

P

Lower
Chippewa
Picnic Area

BRECKSVILLE RESERVATION

82

Chippewa
Creek Falls

Gorge Overlook

Gorge
Loop

Shelter

Gorge Loop

P

Meadows Drive

Small waterfalls downstream of Chippewa Creek Falls

The trail is wide and flat for the most part. As you hike upstream and approach Chippewa Creek Falls, the trail takes you down to the river's edge. Here you see smaller waterfalls, riffles, and pools among the boulders. It's a great place to have lunch and hang out for a while. Despite what you may see, wading and swimming are prohibited.

The trail ends near the parking lot at the Chippewa Creek Gorge Overlook platform. From here you can see a stone arch where SR 82 crosses over the creek. Late fall through early spring you can get a view of Chippewa Creek Falls below the arch. At other times they are a bit obscured, but you have a clear view of the gorge year-round. There are picnic tables here; it's a great spot for a mid-hike lunch.

There are plenty of other things to check out while you're here. Visit the Brecksville Nature Center & Trailside Program Center; next to it is a restored 3-acre prairie (look for monarch butterflies in summer). The nature center offers plenty of programming; check online. During very high water events, there is another waterfall in this reservation, Deer Lick Cave Falls. You're more likely to see evidence of a waterfall in the winter, when ice accumulates. Deer Lick Cave is accessible off the Deer Lick Cave Loop. This spot is named for the naturally occurring salt in the sandstone, which drew deer here.

Miles and Directions

0.0 Start at the Hemlock Trail trailhead, across the road from the Lower Chippewa Creek Drive parking lot. It's marked with a trail sign. In about 500 feet, cross a pedestrian suspension bridge. Some access trails will come in from the left. Stay straight on the wide main trail, paralleling the creek.

0.9 After ascending a hill, pass a trail on the left that leads to the nature center. Continue straight.

1.1 Come to a fork. Take the right fork onto the Gorge Loop and begin descending into the gorge.

1.2 A spur trail on the right takes you down stone steps to Chippewa Creek. Use this trail to access the creek's edge, then return to this spot and turn right to continue upstream.

1.3 Return to the Hemlock Trail at a junction. Turn right and continue upstream. Pass a shelter and an access trail on the left, continuing straight.

1.4 Arrive at the Gorge Overlook. Turn around and return the way you came.

2.8 Arrive back at the trailhead.

Hike Information

Local information: Destination Cleveland; (216) 875-6680; thisiscleveland.com

Hiking groups: Cleveland Hiking Club; clevelandhikingclub.org

Northeast Ohio Hiking Club; meetup.com/NEOHiking/

Camping: The Brecksville Reservation is home to a backpacking campsite, available by reservation only. Learn more at clevelandmetroparks.com/parks/visit/activities/activity-types/backpacking.

7 Linda Falls

Located in Cleveland Metroparks' Bedford Reservation, Linda Falls is usually overlooked in favor of Bedford's Bridal Veil Falls, Great Falls of Tinker's Creek, or Brandywine Falls in the adjacent Cuyahoga Valley National Park. But this is a great add-on: Follow the blue blazes of the Buckeye Trail to Linda Falls in early spring after a good rain—when the water is flowing, the view of the falls is well worth the hike.

Height of falls: About 20 feet
Type of falls: Plunge to cascade
Distance: 2.0 miles out and back
Difficulty: Moderate due to stream crossings
Hiking time: About 1 hour
Trail name: Buckeye Trail
Trail surface: Dirt, asphalt

Seasons and hours: Best late winter and early spring; open daily, 6 a.m. to 11 p.m.
Canine compatibility: Leashed dogs permitted
Trailhead facilities: Porta potty
Trail contact: Cleveland Metroparks Bedford Reservation; (614) 206-1000; cleveland metroparks.com/parks/visit/parks/bedford -reservation

Finding the trailhead: From I-77 exit 153 in Independence, go east on East Pleasant Valley Road for 2.7 miles, where it becomes Alexander Road. Continue another 1.5 miles east to a small trailhead parking lot on the right. Look for a trailhead kiosk on the east end of the parking lot, by the Bike and Hike Trail. GPS: N41 21.28' / W81 34.07'

The Hike

There are so many waterfalls to explore in the Bedford Reservation and the adjacent Cuyahoga Valley National Park. Some are hidden (off-trail and hard to find), some have great access (think Brandywine Falls), and others—like Linda Falls—are hidden in plain sight. Linda Falls may be under the radar, but the cascade is trailside. And the trail that takes you to Linda Falls is the longest and most iconic one in Ohio: the Buckeye Trail.

Begin at the trailhead kiosk near the parking lot off Alexander Road where Cuyahoga and Summit Counties meet. To the north, the paved trail is part of Cleveland Metroparks. Begin by hiking south on the paved trail—here it is the Hike and Bike Trail, which is part of Summit Metroparks. Soon exit the trail and walk down toward Sagamore Run on the footpath that is the Buckeye Trail. As always, follow the blue blazes. The valley created by Sagamore Creek is quite pretty, and a late fall to early spring hike will give you views of the valley. You will cross a side drainage to Sagamore Creek, so be sure to wear waterproof shoes or boots.

Walk through a largely maple-beech forest, which brings brilliant fall colors. In the spring look for wildflowers like trillium, phlox, wild geranium, bloodroot, and

Linda Falls

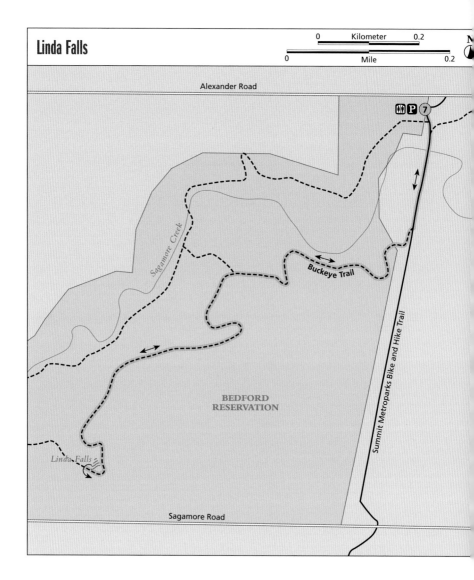

Alexander Road

Sagamore Creek

Buckeye Trail

Summit Metroparks Bike and Hike Trail

BEDFORD
RESERVATION

Linda Falls

Sagamore Road

twinleaf. You can often see wild mushrooms here too. The trail eventually winds its way to another side drainage to Sagamore Creek, where Linda Falls pours into a natural shale amphitheater. Some people call this Twin Sisters Falls because, depending on flow, it can be two distinct waterfalls plunging from opposite sides over the lip, meeting in the stream below. The main flow is on the right side, which can expand to two waterfalls on either side or a single large cataract on the rare occasion that the water is flowing heavily. There is another waterfall in Cuyahoga Valley National Park named Twin Sisters Falls that looks similar to Linda Falls. And if that's not confusing enough, Linda Falls has also been known as Alexander Falls. When water is high, you can view other ephemeral falls in this area.

A sometimes-good option for a longer (3.6-mile) hike is to continue west on the Buckeye Trail to Frazee House in Cuyahoga Valley National Park and make a loop by returning on the bridle trail. However, this longer option is not well marked, can be overgrown, and can be very muddy.

Bedford Reservation gives you a three-fer: In addition to Linda Falls, this "sprawling" metropark is also home to Bridal Veil Falls and Great Falls of Tinker's Creek.

Miles and Directions

0.0 Start from the trailhead kiosk; take a right and walk on the paved Summit Metroparks Bike and Hike Trail (away from Alexander Road).

0.2 Underneath the power lines, exit the paved path and take the Buckeye Trail (not well marked here) down and to the right. Look for blue blazes.

0.5 Arrive at a fork with a connector trail. Take the left fork, looking for the blue blazes.

1.0 Arrive at the top of Linda Falls. Return the way you came.

2.0 Arrive back at the trailhead.

Hike Information

Local information: Destination Cleveland; thisiscleveland.com; (216) 875-6680
Organizations: Buckeye Trail Association; (740) 394-2008; buckeyetrail.org
Hiking groups: Cleveland Hiking Club; clevelandhikingclub.org
Northeast Ohio Hiking Club; meetup.com/NEOHiking/

8 Bridal Veil Falls

It's easy to picture a bride's veil or even a long train on a wedding dress—Bridal Veil Falls cascades more than 100 feet down a chute composed of shale bedrock. The falls are surrounded by a forest of deciduous trees and hemlocks, making this an attractive site any time of year. Hike this popular 3.0-mile section of the statewide Buckeye Trail for a pleasant walk to the falls and then to the Tinker's Creek Gorge Overlook.

Height of falls: About 20 feet high and more than 100 feet long
Type of falls: Cascade
Distance: 3.0-mile one-way shuttle (6.0 miles out and back)
Difficulty: Easy to moderate
Hiking time: About 1.5 hours one way (3 hours out and back)
Trail name: Buckeye Trail
Trail surface: Dirt
Seasons and hours: Best winter and spring; open daily, 6 a.m. to 11 p.m.

Canine compatibility: Leashed dogs permitted
Trailhead facilities: Restrooms, picnic area
Trail contact: Cleveland Metroparks Bedford Reservation; (614) 206-1000; clevelandmetroparks.com/parks/visit/parks/bedford-reservation
Special considerations: This is both a hiking trail and a bridle trail. All trail users should exercise courtesy and caution. Horses have right-of-way.

Finding the trailhead: From I-480 in Bedford, take exit 23 for SR 14/Broadway Avenue/Forbes Road. Drive west on Broadway for 0.9 mile to Egbert Road/Hawthorne Parkway. Take a left and go 0.6 mile to Gorge Parkway. Take a right and go 0.3 mile to the Egbert Picnic Area on the right. GPS: N41 23.04' / W81 32.20'
To shuttle: From the Egbert Picnic Area, continue on Gorge Parkway another 2.4 miles to the Tinker's Creek Gorge Overlook parking area on the right. GPS: N41 22.38' / W81 33.32'

The Hike

This hike is just one short section of the 1,400-mile statewide Buckeye Trail (BT), but it's one of the best sections. A number of formal and social trails converge here, so keep your eyes peeled for the BT's signature blue blazes to stay on track. This section of trail doubles as a hiking trail and a bridle trail. Most junctions are well marked. At times you'll cross mountain bike trails and the paved All Purpose Trail. This dense network of trails is evidence of how popular the Cleveland Metroparks are for many users, from hikers to mountain bikers to horseback riders.

The Bedford Reservation is known for Bridal Veil Falls and the Tinker's Creek Gorge Overlook. This overlook gives you a great view of the nearly 200-foot–deep gorge, which was created after the last glacier retreated some 12,000 years ago. Fall is a great time to take in this overlook, when the forest turns shades of yellow, red, and

Bridal Veil Falls

orange. Be sure to go after a rain, however, because Bridal Veil Falls can be reduced to a trickle during dry weather.

The trail begins at the Egbert Picnic Area, paralleling Tinker's Creek momentarily and then moving away from the creek and gorge. Although the trail largely parallels the All Purpose Trail and Gorge Parkway, it's still a calm, mostly quiet hike. Look for large trees, including maples (which account for the forest's great fall colors) and

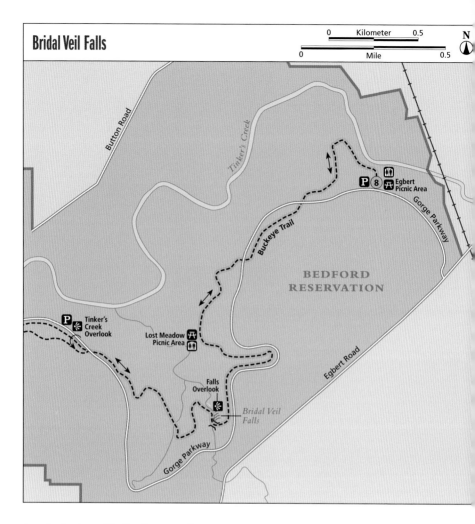

Bridal Veil Falls

0 Kilometer 0.5

0 Mile 0.5

N

Button Road

Tinker's Creek

Buckeye Trail

BEDFORD
RESERVATION

Gorge Parkway

P 8 Egbert
Picnic Area

P Tinker's
Creek
Overlook

Lost Meadow
Picnic Area

Falls
Overlook

Bridal Veil
Falls

Egbert Road

Gorge Parkway

hemlocks (specifically, framing the streams). Spring wildflowers include phlox, mayapple, and bluet.

If it's been raining recently, you'll hear Bridal Veil Falls before you see it. A footbridge crosses over Deerlick Creek, which is a tributary of Tinker's Creek. It's named Deerlick Creek because a natural salt seam has long attracted deer to the creek. An overlook deck gives you a great view of the falls. Depending on how you measure it, the water here cascades for as much as 200 feet. From here the trail moves farther away from the road, giving you a more secluded feel. After it meets up with Gorge Parkway again, you are almost at the Tinker's Creek Gorge Overlook, a great place to end your hike. Tinker's Creek, at more than 28 miles long, is the largest tributary of the Cuyahoga River. Tinker's Creek Gorge is a section of the creek where it drops more than 200 feet in 2 miles. It is registered as a National Natural Landmark.

Nearby and also within the Bedford Reservation are the Great Falls of Tinker's Creek and Linda Falls. While you're in the area, it's worth checking out all three waterfalls.

Bridal Veil Falls

Miles and Directions

0.0 Start at a post for the Buckeye Trail on the northern edge of the Egbert Picnic Area parking lot. A short spur takes you to the BT, where it briefly parallels Tinker's Creek and takes you around the picnic area. The BT follows different trails in this section, so keep an eye out and follow the blue blazes.

0.5 Cross several trails in quick succession, including the All Purpose Trail, and then cross Gorge Parkway. On the other side, come to a junction with the mountain bike trail. Keep right, paralleling Gorge Parkway.

0.9 Cross Gorge Parkway and continue straight.

1.25 Cross an access road to Lost Meadows Picnic Area.

2.0 Cross a footbridge over the stream. In about 100 feet, come to the overlook platform for Bridal Veil Falls. After viewing the falls, continue in the direction you were hiking (downstream).

2.9 Cross Gorge Parkway and come to the All Purpose Trail. Take a right and walk the All Purpose Trail for about 100 yards.

3.0 Cross Gorge Parkway again and walk to the Tinker's Creek Gorge Overlook platform. End here if you shuttled, or return the way you came.

6.0 If you hiked out and back, arrive back at the trailhead.

Hike Information

Local information: Destination Cleveland; (216) 875-6680; thisiscleveland.com
Organizations: Buckeye Trail Association; (740) 394-2008; buckeyetrail.org
Hiking groups: Cleveland Hiking Club; clevelandhikingclub.org
Northeast Ohio Hiking Club; meetup.com/NEOHiking/

9 Great Falls of Tinker's Creek

Welcome to the Niagara Falls of Ohio. In late winter and early spring, when flow is high, water drops with great force across a cataract 80 feet wide. Not surprisingly, these urban falls provided hydropower for a gristmill, a sawmill, and an electric power plant for nearly a century. Today they provide an exceptional green space embedded within urban surroundings.

Height of falls: About 15 feet tall, 80 feet wide
Type of falls: Block
Distance: 0.6-mile lollipop
Difficulty: Easy
Hiking time: About 20 minutes
Trail name: Viaduct Park Loop
Trail surface: Asphalt, dirt
Seasons and hours: Best winter and spring; open daily, 6 a.m. to 11 p.m.

Canine compatibility: Dogs permitted on an 8-foot leash; you must pick up after your pet.
Trailhead facilities: Porta potty
Trail contact: Cleveland Metroparks Bedford Reservation; (216) 635-3200; cleveland metroparks.com/parks/visit/parks/bedford -reservation/great-falls-of-tinker-s-creek

Finding the trailhead: From I-480 near Bedford Heights, take the Broadway/SR 14 exit. Go northwest on Broadway for 1.3 miles to Taylor Road. Look for a "Cleveland Metroparks" sign. Take a left and continue 0.2 mile to Willis Street. Turn left into the parking lot. GPS: N41 23.07' / W81 32.02'

The Hike

Great Falls of Tinker's Creek is surprisingly under the radar compared to famous northeast Ohio waterfalls like Brandywine Falls. It's a must-see waterfall in the Cleveland area. Like all waterfalls, Great Falls of Tinker's Creek is created by a harder rock—Berea Sandstone—not wearing away as quickly as a softer rock below—in this case, Bedford Shale. Stop and look at the interpretive signs along this trail and you'll see old photos showing how the waterfall has "receded" over the years.

Tinker's Creek is the largest tributary of the heavily industrialized Cuyahoga River, and Cleveland's industrial past can also be seen here. By 1825, both a sawmill and gristmill existed along Tinker's Creek. A hydroelectric power plant was opened in 1892. Look for old mill foundations from the falls overlook.

Starting from above at the Viaduct Park parking lot in the Bedford Reservation, follow the paved Viaduct Park Loop; you'll quickly see the namesake viaduct. A viaduct is a bridge with arches that is usually built to support railroad tracks. Viaduct Bridge was built for the Cleveland and Pittsburgh Railroad and completed in 1864. Check out the photo on a trailside interpretive sign to see how tall the viaduct was originally, before much of the creek valley was filled in to support new rail lines.

Great Falls of Tinker's Creek

Below the viaduct is The Arch, another sandstone structure (completed in 1902) built to control the flow of Tinker's Creek, which was impacted by the backfilling required to build the viaduct.

Tinker's Creek (named for Joseph Tinker, a member of Moses Cleaveland's survey crew) forms Tinker's Creek Gorge, a National Natural Landmark. This beautiful, cool valley is home to a deciduous forest plus evergreen hemlock trees. If it weren't for the roar of the waterfall, you could listen for the calls of hawks and woodpeckers.

Miles and Directions

0.0 Start from the small parking lot and walk on the paved trail, passing park benches. Descend into the gorge, staying on the paved trail.

0.2 Begin the loop in a counterclockwise direction and come to two overlooks; the second is the main falls overlook. Continue straight past the overlook, paralleling the creek.

0.4 Loop back to the paved trail, taking stairs to ascend out of the valley.

0.6 Arrive back at the trailhead.

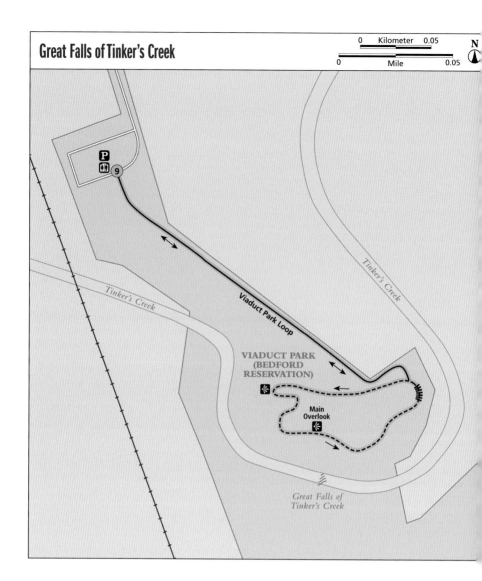

Hike Information

Local information: Destination Cleveland; (216) 875-6680; thisiscleveland.com
Hiking groups: Cleveland Hiking Club; clevelandhikingclub.org
Northeast Ohio Hiking Club; meetup.com/NEOHiking/

10 Blue Hen Falls

Cuyahoga Valley National Park is home to dozens of waterfalls. Most are ephemeral, off-trail, off-map, and difficult to get to. But don't worry, the most beautiful waterfalls are easily accessible. Case in point: the hike to Blue Hen Falls. This photo-ready waterfall is surrounded by dense forest and is accessed along the iconic Buckeye Trail.

Height of falls: 15 feet
Type of falls: Plunge
Distance: 2.6 miles out and back
Difficulty: Moderate due to some steep sections
Hiking time: About 1 hour
Trail name: Buckeye Trail
Trail surface: Dirt
Seasons and hours: Best in spring; open 24/7/365
Canine compatibility: Leashed dogs permitted; you must pick up after your pet.

Trailhead facilities: Visitor center with water and restrooms
Trail contact: Cuyahoga Valley National Park; (330) 657-2752; nps.gov/cuva
   Boston Mill Visitor Center; (440) 717-3890; nps.gov/cuva/boston-mill-visitor-center.htm; open daily, 9:30 a.m. to 5 p.m., except New Year's Day, Thanksgiving, Christmas Eve, and Christmas Day
Special considerations: This is a very popular hike, and the parking lot fills up quickly; go on a weekday if possible.

Finding the trailhead: From I-271 exit 12 in Richfield, go east on SR 303 for 0.2 mile to Stine Road. Turn left (north) onto Stine Road and go 1.6 miles to Riverview Road. Turn left onto Riverview Road and go 1 mile to the Boston Mill Visitor Center parking lot on the right. To get to the trailhead, walk from the visitor center across the railroad tracks and continue to the intersection of Boston Mills and Riverview Roads. Cross Riverview Road and pick up the trailhead, between the road and the woods. GPS: N41 15.44' / W81 3.37'

The Hike

Cuyahoga Valley National Park is one of two regions in Ohio with a high concentration of waterfalls (the other one is the Hocking Hills in southeast Ohio). When the Cuyahoga Valley National Recreation Area was created in 1974, one goal was to bring the parks to the masses. This was a good bet, since the park spans the area between Cleveland and Akron. Upgraded to national park status in 2000, today Cuyahoga Valley National Park sees more than 2 million visitors per year, from both near and far. Waterfall chasing is a popular pastime here.

The park is named for the Cuyahoga River, whose name comes from a variation on *Cayagaga* in the Mohawk language, meaning "crooked river." The Seneca people called it "Cuyohoga." Indeed, the river is crooked, starting east of Cleveland and then flowing south before making a U-turn around Akron and then flowing north to Cleveland—where, yes, it caught fire in 1969 (and several times before that). In addition to the subsequent Clean Water Act—at least partly inspired by the Cuyahoga

Blue Hen Falls

River catching fire—the park has continually improved the environmental quality of the water and land inside its boundaries.

This hike begins near the Cuyahoga River. Park and stop in at the Boston Mill Visitor Center, where you can learn more about the history of the park. Scan the river and see if you can spot a bald eagle, kingfisher, or great blue heron. The Blue Hen

Blue Hen Falls

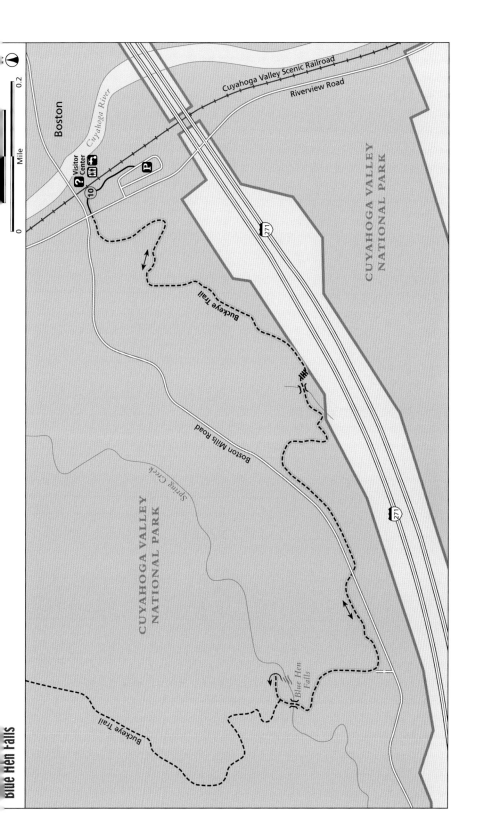

Falls trailhead is west of the visitor center. This hike is on a section of the 1,440-mile, statewide Buckeye Trail and is one of the most iconic sections of the path. Ascend out of the Cuyahoga River valley to the ridgetop, paralleling Boston Mills Road. Cross the road and enter the forest, where the nearby metro areas seem a world away.

Approach Spring Creek, a tributary to the Cuyahoga, and leave the BT to walk downstream on a short spur to Blue Hen Falls. Surrounded by maple trees, this waterfall is Instagram-ready in the fall, when the leaves turn yellow and orange. Blue Hen Falls plunges into a natural amphitheater with a small pool. Spring may be an even better time to do this hike—the water is flowing high, and wildflowers include spring beauty, bloodroot, mayapple, and wild geranium.

Old-timers remember Buttermilk Falls, downstream from here. Those waterfalls are actually located on private property, so please turn around after you've reached Blue Hen Falls.

Miles and Directions

0.0 Start from the Boston Mill Visitor Center and walk to the intersection of Boston Mills and Riverview Roads. Cross Riverview Road and enter the woods on a gravel path.

0.7 The trail approaches Boston Mills Road but does not cross. Parallel the road on the trail.

0.9 Cross Boston Mills Road at a crosswalk.

1.1 Come to a T intersection with an old gravel road and turn right. Walk past an old gravel parking area and a trail kiosk.

1.25 Arrive at a junction. The BT turns left here. Continue straight to Blue Hen Falls.

1.3 Reach Blue Hen Falls. Retrace your steps to the trailhead from here.

2.6 Arrive back at the trailhead.

Hike Information

Local information: Akron/Summit Convention & Visitors Bureau; (800) 245-4254; visitakron-summit.org

Destination Cleveland; (800) 245-4254; thisiscleveland.com

Organizations: Conservancy for Cuyahoga Valley National Park; (330) 657-2909; conservancyforcvnp.org

Cuyahoga Valley Trails Council; cvtrailscouncil.org

Buckeye Trail Association; (740) 394-2008; buckeyetrail.org

Hiking groups: Cleveland Hiking Club; clevelandhikingclub.org

Northeast Ohio Hiking Club; meetup.com/NEOHiking/

Greater Akron Area Hikers: meetup.com/summit_county_ohio_hikers/

Camping: The adjacent Cleveland Metroparks Brecksville Reservation has backpacking campsites available by reservation only. For more information go to cleveland metroparks.com/parks/visit/activities/activity-types/backpacking.

11 Brandywine Falls

Sixty-foot-tall Brandywine Falls is likely the most famous and popular waterfall in Ohio. And why not—the beautiful cascade has reliable flow, great viewing infrastructure, and plenty of hiking options right around it. It's a centerpiece of Cuyahoga Valley National Park. Start with Brandywine Falls and then explore some more of the waterfalls and trails in Ohio's only national park.

Height of falls: 60 feet
Type of falls: Cascade
Distance: 1.5-mile loop
Difficulty: Easy
Hiking time: About 45 minutes
Trail name: Brandywine Gorge Loop
Trail surface: Boardwalk, dirt, asphalt
Seasons and hours: Good year-round, best on weekdays; open 24/7/365
Canine compatibility: Leashed dogs permitted; you must pick up after your pet.
Trailhead facilities: Water, restrooms, picnic area

Trail contact: Cuyahoga Valley National Park; (330) 657-2752; nps.gov/cuva
   Boston Mill Visitor Center; (440) 717-3890; nps.gov/cuva/boston-mill-visitor-center.htm; open daily, 9:30 a.m. to 5 p.m., except for New Year's Day, Thanksgiving, Christmas Eve, and Christmas Day
Special considerations: This is an extremely popular hike, and the parking lot fills up very quickly. If possible, plan to go on a weekday, the earlier the better.

Finding the trailhead: From I-77 exit 149/149A, go east on SR 82 for 5.6 miles to South Boyden Road. Turn right (south) onto South Boyden Road and continue 1.6 miles to West Highland Road. Turn left and go 0.5 mile to Brandywine Road. Turn right and go 1.1 miles to the parking lot on the right. GPS: N41 16.35' / W81 32.24'

The Hike

Brandywine Falls is one of the most, if not the most, recognizable attraction of Cuyahoga Valley National Park. Tumbling along Brandywine Creek, even the names of the rock that create the conditions for this waterfall are quintessential northeast Ohio: The water tumbles over the harder Berea Sandstone and has worn away the softer Bedford and Cleveland Shales to create the cascading falls.

The first portion of the hike is a direct path to the falls. A wheelchair-accessible boardwalk goes all the way to the upper viewing platform. For the able-bodied, don't miss the steps down to the lower viewing platform, which take you close enough to the falls to feel the mist on your face when the flow is high. One attraction of this hike is how often you are within eyeshot and earshot of the water.

The trail then makes a loop around the other side of Brandywine Creek, which is a tributary of the Cuyahoga River. Hike down into the gorge, cross the gorge on a footbridge, then come back out. Look and listen for the songs of red-winged

Brandywine Falls

blackbirds, cedar waxwings, juncos, and many more birds. Other wildlife include squirrels and white-tailed deer. Spring brings wildflowers like trillium, Dutchman's breeches, and mayapple. Fall is brilliant with yellow maple leaves falling onto the forest floor and into the water.

There is another named waterfall nearby. Near the footbridge that spans Brandy-wine Creek is a side drainage waterfall called Shredder Falls. It gets its named supposedly from Boy Scouts who, back in the day, would slide down the cascade, shredding their shorts.

If you are looking for more mileage, no problem. The Summit Metro Parks Bike & Hike Trail intersects the Brandywine Gorge Loop and is a total of 34 miles in length. The Brandywine Gorge Loop connects with the Stanford Trail, which goes 1.5 miles south to Stanford House. The historic Stanford House is operated by the Conservancy for Cuyahoga Valley National Park and is available for rent for meetings or for overnight stays.

The only downside to this hike is that its popularity makes parking difficult, especially on weekends. Try to plan your hike for a weekday if possible. Even then, arriving early is a good idea.

Brandywine Falls

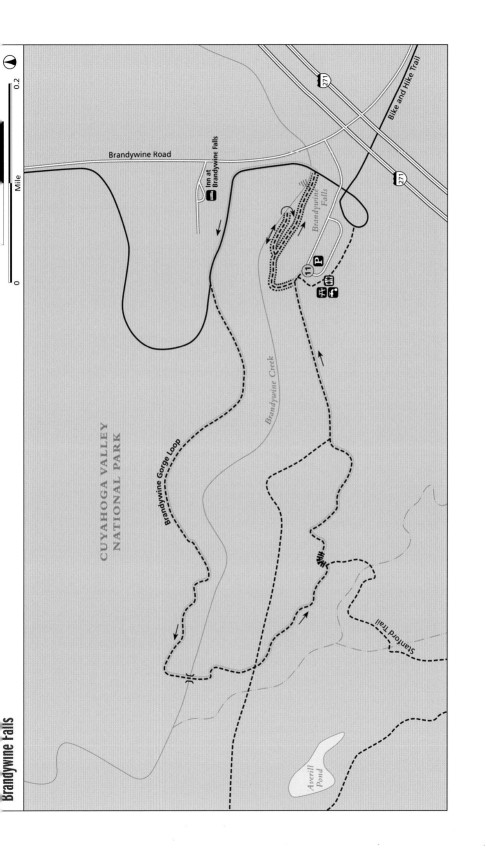

CUYAHOGA VALLEY NATIONAL PARK

Brandywine Gorge Loop

Brandywine Creek

Averill Pond

Stanford Trail

Brandywine Road

Inn at Brandywine Falls

Brandywine Falls

11

P

271

271

Bike and Hike Trail

Mile
0   0.2

Another option for getting to Brandywine Falls is to start at the Boston Mill Visitor Center and hike to the falls and back for a 5.0-mile round-trip hike.

Miles and Directions

0.0 Start at the west end of the parking lot. Pick up the trailhead, marked with a sign for Brandywine Falls. In about 50 feet, pass a junction with the Stanford Trail. Continue straight, onto the boardwalk. In about 350 feet, come to a junction. Turn left and descend the steps down to the first (lower) Brandywine Falls overlook.

0.1 Arrive at the overlook. Turn around and return to the junction. Once back at the junction at the top of the stairs, turn left.

0.2 Arrive at the second, upper, overlook. Continue straight past the overlook. The boardwalk ends here.

0.3 Come to a T intersection with the paved bike path. Turn left and walk along the pavement.

0.5 Exit the paved path to the left and join the dirt path.

1.0 Cross Brandywine Creek on a footbridge. After crossing, the trail trends left (upstream).

1.1 Cross a decommissioned road.

1.2 Arrive at the junction with the Stanford Trail. Turn left, following the sign for Brandywine Falls, and hike out of the gorge.

1.3 Come to a junction with the decommissioned road you crossed earlier. Turn right and follow the road, which becomes a gravel path.

1.5 Arrive back at the trailhead.

Hike Information

Local information: Akron/Summit Convention & Visitors Bureau; (800) 245-4254; visitakron-summit.org

Destination Cleveland; (216) 875-6680; thisiscleveland.com

Organizations: Conservancy for Cuyahoga Valley National Park; (330) 657-2909; conservancyforcvnp.org

Cuyahoga Valley Trails Council; cvtrailscouncil.org

Hiking groups: Cleveland Hiking Club; clevelandhikingclub.org

Northeast Ohio Hiking Club; meetup.com/NEOHiking/

Greater Akron Area Hikers; meetup.com/summit_county_ohio_hikers/

Camping: The adjacent Cleveland Metroparks Brecksville Reservation has backpacking campsites available by reservation only. For more information go to cleveland metroparks.com/parks/visit/activities/activity-types/backpacking.

12 Sulphur Springs Falls

This is as close to a great creeking hike as you'll get in the Cleveland Metroparks. Sulphur Springs is a creek full of small cascades, and this hike includes three stream crossings. Bring your water shoes, or plan to go barefoot. Take a moment to explore Sulphur Springs as you cross it. Listen to a lively bird population, and look for a wide variety of spring wildflowers.

Height of falls: 6 feet
Type of falls: Cascade
Distance: 2.4-mile lollipop
Difficulty: Moderate due to stream crossings
Hiking time: About 1.5 hours
Trail names: Bridle Trail, Sulphur Springs Loop, Buckeye Trail
Trail surface: Crushed gravel, dirt
Seasons and hours: Best late spring and early summer; open daily, 6 a.m. to 11 p.m.

Canine compatibility: Leashed dogs permitted
Trailhead facilities: Vault toilet
Trail contact: Cleveland Metroparks South Chagrin Reservation; (440) 473-3370; clevelandmetroparks.com/parks/visit/parks/south-chagrin-reservation
Special considerations: This hike requires creek crossings; exercise good judgment based on water conditions.

Finding the trailhead: From US 422 in Solon, turn north on SOM Center Road. Go 1.4 miles to Hawthorn Parkway, where there is a large "South Chagrin Reservation" sign. Turn right and go 1 mile to Sulphur Springs Drive. Turn left and go 0.7 mile to parking at the junction of Sulphur Springs Drive and Chagrin River Road. The trailhead is on the north side of Sulphur Springs Road, across the road from the big "South Chagrin Reservation" sign. GPS: N41 25.23' / W81 25.04'

The Hike

Beginning on the Bridle Trail, you'll approach Sulphur Springs, a tributary of the Chagrin River, in just a couple hundred feet. Immediately you'll be met with the sounds and—if you look at the creek closely—a view of the first cascade you'll encounter on this hike. The cascades along this creek are quite attractive but modest, so a late-spring/early-summer outing is best, when water levels are generally higher. Better yet, go after a good rain. Spring brings a plethora of showy wildflowers, including bloodroot, jack-in-the-pulpit, wild geranium, foamflower, bluet, and more. Hemlocks line the creek, and the forest also includes maple, beech, and mature oak trees. There are plenty of ferns along this trail as well.

As you walk upstream, you'll leave the wide gravel Bridle Trail for a singletrack dirt path. Again, you'll walk by lively cascades on Sulphur Springs, audible and visible from the trail, though a bit obscured by the forest. Soon you'll approach the Sulphur Springs Picnic Area. Before the main picnic area, you'll come across a few dispersed picnic tables near the cascades. This would make an ideal lunch spot.

A waterfall along Sulphur Springs

Near the picnic area parking area, pick up the Sulphur Springs Loop. This marks your first required stream crossing of the hike. Bring a walking stick or trekking poles, water shoes (or go barefoot), and have fun crossing the creek here. Upstream is the largest cascade on the creek, informally known as Sulphur Springs Falls. As you complete the loop (which returns to this point, taking you right past the falls), you will cross the creek two more times.

This is a great birding hike as well. Listen for the lively chickadees, cardinals, woodpeckers, and more birds that call this riparian area home. You'll also have a chance to hike a small portion of the Buckeye Trail, a statewide 1,400-mile loop.

An even better place to start in the South Chagrin Reservation is the hike to Quarry Rock and Double Decker Falls. And just a couple of miles away is Chagrin Falls, the waterfall for which the town is named. Chagrin Falls is right downtown—no hiking required.

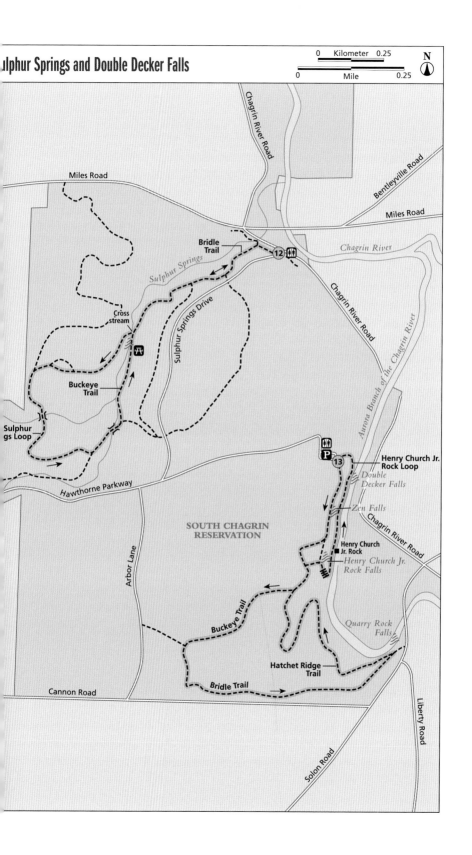

0   Kilometer   0.25

0   Mile   0.25

N

Chagrin River Road

Bentleyville Road

Miles Road

Miles Road

Bridle Trail

Chagrin River

12

Sulphur Springs

Chagrin River Road

Cross stream

Sulphur Springs Drive

Aurora Branch of the Chagrin River

Buckeye Trail

Henry Church Jr. Rock Loop

P

13

Double Decker Falls

Sulphur gs Loop

Zen Falls

Hawthorne Parkway

Chagrin River Road

SOUTH CHAGRIN RESERVATION

Henry Church Jr. Rock

Henry Church Jr. Rock Falls

Arbor Lane

Buckeye Trail

Quarry Rock Falls

Hatchet Ridge Trail

Cannon Road

Bridle Trail

Solon Road

Liberty Road

Miles and Directions

0.0 Start at the Miles Road Sledding Hill. Start by the large "South Chagrin Reservation" sign at the intersection of Sulphur Springs Drive and Chagrin River Road. Cross Sulphur Springs road and pick up the gravel Bridle Trail, marked with a trail post. In about 200 feet, come to a junction. (There are small, cascading falls here). Turn left.

0.2 Come to a junction with a trail on the left. Continue straight on the Bridle Trail.

0.3 Where the Bridle Trail crosses the road, do not cross. Instead, turn right and pick up a singletrack trail that parallels the road. Look and listen for a series of cascading falls along this section of creek.

0.4 Pass some picnic tables and a fire ring on the right, and come to a fork. Take the left fork; pass a trail post and see double blue blazes for the Buckeye Trail (BT) straight ahead.

0.6 Come to a junction with an orange hiker blaze on a tree. Turn right and wade across Sulphur Springs. This begins the loop. The trail ascends out of the valley on a decommissioned road.

0.8 The trail/road forks and comes back together. Where it comes back together, continue straight onto a gravel road.

1.0 Come to a junction with the Bridle Trail at a post with an orange hiker blaze and Bridle Trail blaze. Turn left.

1.1 Wade across the stream again.

1.5 Arrive at a T intersection. Turn left, still on the Bridle Trail. In a few hundred feet, make another stream crossing.

1.6 Come to a fork. Take the left fork, joining the BT again on singletrack trail.

1.8 Arrive at Sulphur Springs Picnic Area parking. The BT skirts the parking lot to the left. This is where a small cascade is located on the creek, the one known informally as Sulphur Springs Falls. Continue walking downstream to the junction where you began the loop. Continue straight and retrace your steps to the trailhead.

2.4 Arrive back at the trailhead.

Hike Information

Local information: Destination Cleveland; (216) 875-6680; thisiscleveland.com
Organizations: Buckeye Trail Association; (740) 394-2008; buckeyetrail.org
Hiking groups: Cleveland Hiking Club; clevelandhikingclub.org
Northeast Ohio Hiking Club; meetup.com/NEOHiking/

13 Double Decker and Quarry Rock Falls

If you could select only one trail in northeast Ohio to experience Cleveland Metroparks, the statewide Buckeye Trail, and numerous waterfalls, this hike would be your best bet. Two voluminous and beautiful waterfalls drop along the Aurora Branch of the Chagrin River, and several small tributary waterfalls are visible from the same trail. This 3.1-mile hike takes you past all of them. Walk a section of the Buckeye Trail, view Quarry Rock Falls from above, see the locally famous Henry Church Jr. Rock, and end by the trailside Double Decker Falls. **(See map on page 67.)**

Height of falls: 6–10 feet tall, 50-plus feet wide

Type of falls: Plunge

Distance: 3.1-mile double loop

Difficulty: Moderate due to length and stairs

Hiking time: About 1.5 hours

Trail names: Buckeye Trail, Bridle Trail, Hatchet Ridge Trail, Henry Church Jr. Rock Loop

Trail surface: Dirt

Seasons and hours: Best late spring and early summer; open daily, 6 a.m. to 11 p.m.

Canine compatibility: Leashed dogs permitted

Trailhead facilities: Vault toilet, fire pit

Trail contact: Cleveland Metroparks South Chagrin Reservation; (440) 473-3370; clevelandmetroparks.com/parks/visit/parks/south-chagrin-reservation

Finding the trailhead: From US 422 in Solon, turn north on SOM Center Road. Go 1.4 miles to Hawthorn Parkway, where there is a large "South Chagrin Reservation" sign. Turn right and go another 1.4 miles, where the road ends at the Henry Church Jr. Rock Picnic Area on the right. GPS: N41 24.59' / W81 24.54'

The Hike

Start from the Henry Church Jr. Rock Picnic Area and pick up the Buckeye Trail at the southeast corner of the parking lot. Henry Church Jr. (1836–1908) was a blacksmith and folk artist who lived in Chagrin Falls. His most famous legacy is his "long-term, ephemeral" piece of art: a rock carving by the river here that features a woman, an eagle, a quiver, and a papoose. You may have heard this sculpture called "Squaw Rock," now considered an outdated and offensive term that disparages Native American women. The term "squaw" has appropriately been phased out by Cleveland Metroparks and anyone who desires to leave racial slurs in the past.

Walk along a section of the 1,400-mile statewide Buckeye Trail until you peel off to join the Bridle Trail. As you walk closer to the ridgetop above the river, you'll hear Quarry Rock Falls before you see it. Leave the Bridle Trail and switch back, paralleling the river. You'll view Quarry Rock Falls from above, seeing how the waterfall spans the entire width of the river. The falls are named for a nearby sandstone quarry. Another named waterfall, Majestic Falls, is nearby but not visible from the trail.

Double Decker Falls

As you join the Henry Church Jr. Rock Loop, the trail takes you down to the water's edge. As the trail continues downstream, find ephemeral waterfalls to your left, including Henry Church Jr. Falls, near Henry Church Jr. Rock, and Zen Falls. Spring wildflowers include trout lily and mayapple. Hemlock trees and ferns grow throughout this hike. Additionally, black birch trees are common here. End at Double Decker Falls, another sizable waterfall that spans the river and drops precipitously. As the name implies, it is a two-tiered waterfall that spans the river. Despite what you might see in the summer, swimming is not allowed. From here, hike out of the river valley back to the northeast corner of the parking lot.

If you have time, be sure to also check out Sulphur Springs, a small stream with several small waterfalls. Nearby is Chagrin Falls, the waterfall for which the town was named. It's right in the center of town, so there is no hike involved.

Miles and Directions

0.0 Start by the sign for the Henry Church Rock overlook. Walk south on an asphalt trail, following the blue blazes for the Buckeye Trail.

0.2 Where the asphalt ends, come to a junction. Turn right, staying on the BT.

0.3 Come to a junction with a trail on the left. Continue straight. You're walking a cinder road at this point.

0.7 Come to a four-way junction. The park maintenance facility is straight ahead. Turn left onto the wide, gravel Bridle Trail. (The BT exits to the right here.)

1.5 Before the Bridle Trail crosses the road, and as you hear Quarry Rock Falls below, look for a junction with a singletrack trail on the left. Make a switchback to the left and begin walk-

Quarry Rock Falls

ing downstream, at first paralleling the Bridle Trail. Look for blazes on this trail—metal hiker blazes tacked to the trees fairly high up. The trail is unsigned, but this is the Hatchet Ridge Trail.

2.2 Arrive at a T intersection with the BT back at the cinder road. Turn right.

2.3 At a fork, take the right fork, leaving the BT. In about 100 yards, come to a T intersection. Turn right and then arrive at the top of stone steps. Take the steps down into the gorge, all the way to the river. You are now on Henry Church Jr. Rock Trail.

2.5 After exploring the river's edge, turn back and walk downstream, staying in the gorge and paralleling the river.

2.7 Arrive at a waterfall to the left, at the top of stone steps. Take the steps down to the water and look left to see the falls again. This is Henry Church Jr Rock Falls. From here, look back and to the right to see the Henry Church Jr. Rock.

2.8 Look up and left to see the ephemeral Zen Falls.

3.0 Arrive at Double Decker Falls along the river. After exploring the falls, hike the trail up and out of the gorge.

3.1 Arrive at the parking lot near the trailhead where you began.

Hike Information

Local information: Destination Cleveland; (216) 875-6680; thisiscleveland.com
Organizations: Buckeye Trail Association; (740) 394-2008; buckeyetrail.org
Hiking groups: Cleveland Hiking Club; clevelandhikingclub.org
Northeast Ohio Hiking Club; meetup.com/NEOHiking/

14 Affelder Falls

Spring is the time to visit The West Woods for the ephemeral Affelder Falls—which can have big flow after snowmelt or rain—plus showy spring wildflowers like trillium and trout lily. Any time of year, this popular park is home to a nice nature center with plenty of programming, including occasional naturalist-led hikes to normally off-limits portions of the park. If you plan ahead, you can even camp here.

Height of falls: 20 feet
Type of falls: Plunge, ephemeral
Distance: 4.8 miles out and back
Difficulty: Moderate due to length
Hiking time: 2–2.5 hours
Trail names: Pioneer Bridle Trail, Affelder Link, Waterfall Trail
Trail surface: Crushed gravel, dirt
Seasons and hours: Best late winter and early spring; open daily, 6 a.m. to 11 p.m.; nature center open daily, 10 a.m. to 4:30 p.m.
Canine compatibility: Leashed dogs permitted

Trailhead facilities: None
Trail contact: The West Woods, Geauga Park District; (440) 286-9516; geaugaparkdistrict.org/park/the-west-woods
The West Woods Nature Center; (440) 286-9516; geaugaparkdistrict.org/park/the-west-woods
Special considerations: This is both a hiking trail and a bridle trail. All trail users should exercise courtesy and caution. Horses have right-of-way.

Finding the trailhead: From I-271 exit 29 in Beachwood, take SR 87 east (it goes through a roundabout and makes some turns but is well signed; look out for signs) 8.2 miles to SR 306. From the junction of SR 87 and SR 306 at a light, continue on SR 87/Kinsman Road another 1.8 miles to The West Woods entrance on the right. Turn right (south) into the entrance; in about 100 feet a parking lot/horse staging area is on the right. The trailhead begins near a kiosk at the far end of the parking lot. GPS: N41 27.44' / W81 18.19'

The Hike

This hike begins on the Pioneer Horse Trail, a wide, well-constructed trail specifically designed to handle horse traffic, so it is in good shape and not subject to muddy sections. Enjoy a relatively flat hike where you don't have to watch your feet constantly. Instead, enjoy the maple-beech forest with areas of white pine plus wildflowers like skunk cabbage. It feels pretty far away from it all, except for the traffic noise from Kinsman Road. But then the hike veers away from the road and you can enjoy the quiet woods for the rest of the hike. Pass through a marshy area with cattails, ferns, and towering sycamore trees.

Horses have the right-of-way, so be prepared to give it to them; and if you have a dog, be sure to keep it on a leash and don't scare the horses. It can be nice to hike alongside these beautiful creatures, but be sure to watch out for horse poop. The wide trails are very easy to follow, and junctions are marked with trail signs.

Affelder Falls

Affelder Falls

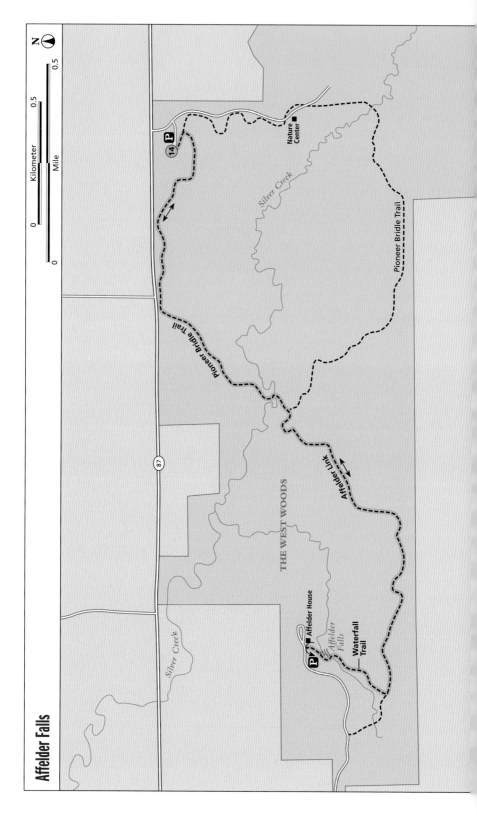

N

Kilometer
0   0.5

Mile
0   0.5

87

14 P

P

Silver Creek

Silver Creek

Nature Center

Pioneer Bridle Trail

Pioneer Bridle Trail

Affelder Link

THE WEST WOODS

Affelder House

Affelder Falls

Waterfall Trail

The final leg of the hike is the Falls Trail, which takes you to Affelder Falls. The forest around the falls is full of spectacularly dense spring wildflowers, including foamflower, wild geranium, Solomon's seal, bloodroot, trillium, and trout lily. If you just want a quick visit to the falls, that's possible too. There is a trailhead just a few hundred feet from the falls, at the Lewis & Ruth Affelder House parking area off SR 306/Chillicothe Road.

While you're here, plan to make a stop at the nature center, which is open daily. You can start and end at the nature center and hike the Pioneer Bridle Trail south and then west to join the Affelder Link before continuing to the falls. The nature center features windows overlooking a large bird feeding area. Look for plentiful common birds like cardinal, chickadee, tufted titmouse, and several species of woodpecker. October through April you can pick up birdseed at the nature center and hike the Trout Lily Trail to the "Bird in the Hand" station, where you cover the bird feeder and the birds will come to your hand to eat the birdseed. Search #geaugaparkdistrict on Instagram to see it in action.

The West Woods—named for an 1885 story set here, "The Young Sugar Makers of the West Woods"—also offers naturalist-led hikes that take you to places not normally open to visitors, like Ansel's Cave. Check the website for programming information. You can also camp on-site; see below for details.

Miles and Directions

0.0 Start at the gravel trail by the trailhead kiosk and walk into the woods. In about 200 feet, come to a marked junction. Turn right and walk the Pioneer Bridle Trail.

1.1 After crossing a footbridge, arrive at a marked junction. Turn right and begin hiking on the Affelder Link.

2.1 Come to a marked junction with the Falls Trail. Turn right.

2.3 Arrive at Affelder Falls. After checking out the falls, backtrack to just above the falls and cross the footbridge.

2.4 The trail ends at the access road to the Lewis & Ruth Affelder House and trailhead parking. Retrace your steps.

4.8 Arrive back at the trailhead.

Hike Information

Local information: Destination Geauga; (440) 632-1538; destinationgeauga.com
Organizations: Foundation for Geauga Parks; (440) 564-1048; foundationforgeauga parks.org
Hiking groups: Geauga Joggers and Walkers hosts walks at The West Woods; npower services.com/geauga.
Camping: Camping is available at The West Woods by reservation only, at least one week in advance. The campsite fills quickly, so plan ahead; reservations.geaugapark district.org/camping.

15 Buttermilk Falls

Hike to Buttermilk Falls in the company of birds, beavers, frogs, turtles, squirrels, and other wildlife. Starting at a nice nature center, walk through a wetland and then a forest to the picturesque and popular falls. Continue downstream for a few more unnamed falls on this varied and pleasant hike.

Height of falls: About 20 feet
Type of falls: Cascade
Distance: 2.5-mile lollipop
Difficulty: Easy
Hiking time: About 1 hour
Trail names: Buttermilk Falls Trail, Hickory Fox Loop, connector trails
Trail surface: Dirt, boardwalk, asphalt
Seasons and hours: Good year-round after a rain; open daily, 6 a.m. to 11 p.m.
Canine compatibility: Leashed dogs permitted

Trailhead facilities: Nature center, restrooms, water, picnic tables
Trail contact: Cleveland Metroparks North Chagrin Reservation; (440) 473-3370; clevelandmetroparks.com/parks/visit/parks/north-chagrin-reservation
North Chagrin Nature Center; (440) 473-3370; clevelandmetroparks.com/parks/visit/parks/north-chagrin-reservation/north-chagrin-nature-center; open daily, 9:30 a.m. to 5 p.m., except for New Year's Day, Thanksgiving, Christmas Eve, and Christmas Day

Finding the trailhead: From I-271 in Mayfield Heights, take exit 36 for Wilson Mills Road. Go east 0.3 mile to SOM Center Road. Turn left (north) and go 2.1 miles to Sunset Lane, which has a large sign for North Chagrin Reservation. Turn right and go 0.2 mile to a T intersection at Buttermilk Falls Parkway. Turn right (then keep right at the fork) and go 0.4 mile to the North Chagrin Nature Center parking on the right. From the parking lot, walk toward the nature center and pick up the trail in front of the nature center. GPS: N41 33.41' / W81 26.07'

The Hike

It's perfect that this hike begins at the North Chagrin Nature Center. Live animal displays include turtles and fish. In addition, there are taxidermied animals and educational displays. Check the North Chagrin website for info about naturalist-led programs. The hike begins by taking you around and over, via boardwalk, Sanctuary Marsh. Look and listen for water-loving birds like red-winged blackbirds, great blue herons, ducks, and geese. Look closely and you may find frogs, turtles, and beavers. Peak bloom for water lilies in the marsh is July. Water-loving plants include swamp white oak, sycamore, and buttonbush.

After leaving the marsh, enter a young forest. In less than 0.5 mile you'll arrive at Buttermilk Falls, which is located on Buttermilk Creek, a tributary of the Chagrin River. The falls pour over blocky chunks of Cleveland Shale, making this a visually distinctive cascade. A stone foundation and wooden bridge spans the creek over the falls, making the overlook a nice spot for a photo year-round—from winter snow to

…termilk Falls in the North Chagrin Reservation

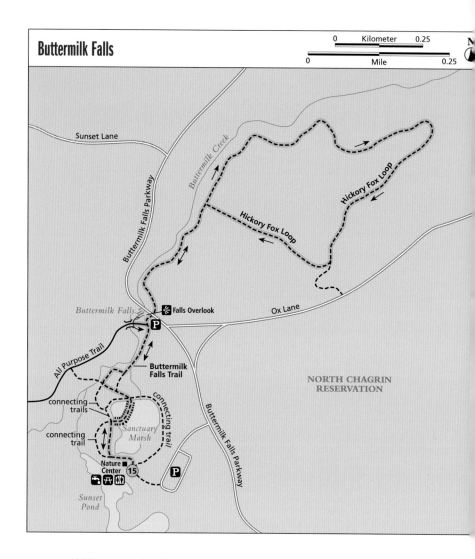

0　　Kilometer　0.25

0　　Mile　　0.25

Sunset Lane

Buttermilk Creek

Buttermilk Falls Parkway

Hickory Fox Loop

Hickory Fox Loop

Buttermilk Falls　◀ Falls Overlook

P

Ox Lane

All Purpose Trail

**Buttermilk
Falls Trail**

connecting
trails

connecting trail

**NORTH CHAGRIN
RESERVATION**

connecting
trail

*Sanctuary
Marsh*

Buttermilk Falls Parkway

Nature ■
Center (15)

P

*Sunset
Pond*

spring wildflowers to fall foliage. This waterfall can easily drain down to a trickle, so be sure to go when the water is high after recent rain.

After viewing the falls, cross Buttermilk Falls Parkway and jump on the Hickory Fox Loop. The blaze for this trail is a squirrel—appropriate, considering the black squirrels that abound along this section of trail. There are more cascading waterfalls along this section of stream. Look down into the gorge to see them, but you will more easily hear them.

While you're at the North Chagrin Reservation, check out the nineteenth-century Squire's Castle, one of the most popular attractions in this park. Finally, this waterfall is not to be confused with Buttermilk Falls near Cuyahoga Valley National Park's Blue Hen Falls. Buttermilk is a popular name for waterfalls—the two in Ohio certainly aren't the only ones—presumably because the churning water reminded people of churning butter.

Miles and Directions

0.0 Start in front of the nature center at a four-way asphalt trail junction. Facing the nature center, turn right and walk about 50 feet to a T intersection. Turn left and walk about 250 feet to a four-way junction. Turn right.

0.1 Arrive at another four-way junction. Turn right and cross the marsh on a boardwalk.

0.2 At the end of the boardwalk, come to a staggered junction. Turn left then right onto a trail marked with a sign reading "To Buttermilk Falls." The trail becomes dirt here, and the trail blaze is a dragonfly. You'll come to a fork; the right one is a shortcut to Buttermilk Falls. Take the left fork, then come to a four-way junction signed for Buttermilk Falls Trail. Turn right.

0.3 Come to a T intersection with the shortcut trail. Turn left.

0.4 Arrive at a junction with the All Purpose Trail. Turn left and walk about 100 feet to the Buttermilk Falls overlook. Return to this junction and turn left to walk across Buttermilk Falls Parkway. Across the road is a four-way junction. Turn left and walk to a sign for the Hickory Fox Loop. The trail trends to the right at this sign. The trail blaze is a squirrel.

0.7 Arrive at a junction with the Castle Valley Connector to the right. Continue straight.

1.5 Come to a second junction with the Castle Valley Connector. Turn right to stay on the Hickory Fox Loop.

1.8 Return to the original junction of the Hickory Fox Loop and Castle Valley Connector. Turn left and retrace your steps to the trailhead.

2.5 Arrive back at the trailhead.

Hike Information

Local information: Destination Cleveland; (216) 875-6680; thisiscleveland.com
Hiking groups: Cleveland Hiking Club; clevelandhikingclub.org
Northeast Ohio Hiking Club; meetup.com/NEOHiking/

16 Stoney Brook Falls

Penitentiary Gorge was so named due to a gorge so steep that it was practically impossible to "escape" it. Today, established trails and steps take you into the gorge to Stoney Brook Falls, making this a great escape from everyday life. Be sure to check the schedule for guided hikes to get a chance to view multiple waterfalls in the gorge. Add in a nature play area and interactive exploration packs for checkout, and this is a great waterfall hike for the whole family.

Height of falls: 10 feet
Type of falls: Cascade
Distance: 1.2-mile loop
Difficulty: Moderate due to steep ascent out of gorge
Hiking time: About 45 minutes
Trail name: Gorge Rim Loop Trail
Trail surface: Dirt, gravel

Seasons and hours: Best in late winter and spring; open daily, 6 a.m. to 11 p.m.
Canine compatibility: Leashed dogs permitted
Trailhead facilities: Nature center, restrooms, water, picnic area, nature play area
Trail contact: Lake Metroparks Penitentiary Glen Reservation; (440) 256-1404; lake metroparks.com/parks-trails/penitentiary-glen -reservation

Finding the trailhead: From I-90 east of Cleveland, take exit 193 to SR 306 South. Go 0.8 mile to a light at Chillicothe Road. Turn left and go 0.2 mile to Kirtland-Chardon Road. Turn right and go 1.9 miles to the Penitentiary Glen Reservation entrance on the right. From the parking lot, follow signs for the nature play area. At the nature play area just past a vault toilet, pick up the Gorge Rim Loop Trail, marked with a sign. GPS: N41 36.44' / W81 19.57'

The Hike

Penitentiary Glen Reservation is a great hiking destination for children of all ages. In addition to a nature play area, nature center, and a miniature steam engine passenger railroad, you can check out an X-Plorer Pack with tools to help your family identify birds, bugs, and more. The Penitentiary Glen Nature Center is open daily, 9 a.m. to 5 p.m.; 9 a.m. to noon Christmas Eve and New Year's Eve; closed Thanksgiving Day and Christmas Day.

Then there's Penitentiary Gorge itself and a number of waterfalls that cascade through it. In all, there are five named waterfalls along Stoney Brook in Penitentiary Glen Reservation. The park regularly offers guided hikes, during which you can view all the falls. It's worth planning ahead in order to be able to attend one of these hikes.

The self-guided Gorge Rim Loop Trail takes you down to Stoney Brook Falls at one of the nicest areas in the gorge, defined by a contrast of rugged (sandstone walls) and delicate, like the spring wildflowers that grow along the trails here, including

Stoney Brook Falls Attila Horvath ▶

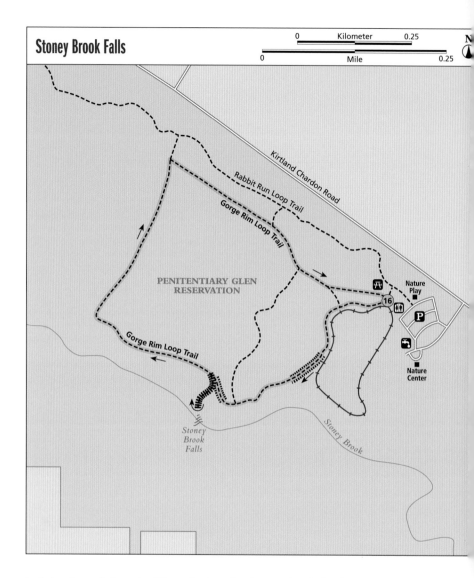

0   Kilometer   0.25

N

0   Mile   0.25

Kirtland Chardon Road

Rabbit Run Loop Trail

Gorge Rim Loop Trail

PENITENTIARY GLEN
RESERVATION

Nature
Play

16

Gorge Rim Loop Trail

Nature
Center

Stoney
Brook
Falls

Stoney Brook

jack-in-the-pulpit and trillium. Spring also brings the flash of redbud trees in bloom. Hemlock trees thrive in the cool, wet gorge area.

The Gorge Rim Loop Trail is mostly flat. But to access the gorge, you hike down more than one hundred steep steps. The payoff is worth it. Water flows through the steep-walled, hemlock-lined gorge. It's attractive in all seasons. At the bottom is the Gorge Trail, which you can access on a guided hike and where you can see more waterfalls upstream. These can be low-flow waterfalls in summer, so plan to come in late winter or spring, or after a good rain.

In the early 1900s, the Halle family of Halle's department store in Cleveland bought the property and ran it as a family summer retreat and farm. Lake Metroparks purchased the property in 1975 and opened it as Penitentiary Glen Reservation in

1980. The name of today's Halle Home Trail is a nod to this history. All told, there are 8.5 miles of trail here, so it's worth exploring more trails during your day at the reservation or coming back for a repeat visit. Even better, plan ahead and reserve the on-site campsite for an overnighter.

Miles and Directions

0.0 Start on the gravel Gorge Rim Loop Trail, walking away from the nature play area. In about 400 feet, come to a fork. Take the left fork to begin the loop.

0.1 Before crossing a set of railroad tracks, turn right and walk on the boardwalk.

0.3 At a junction with the Gorge Rim Connector Trail on the right, continue straight on the Gorge Rim Loop Trail.

0.4 Come to a junction and turn left. Take the stairs down into the gorge and to Stoney Brook Falls. After checking out the falls, hike back up the stairs.

0.5 At the top of the stairs, turn left.

0.9 Come to a junction with the Rabbit Run Loop Trail. Turn right to stay on the Gorge Rim Loop Trail.

1.1 Pass the Gorge Rim Connector on the right and continue straight. Arrive back at the original fork in the trail. This time take a left.

1.2 Arrive back at the trailhead.

Hike Information

Local information: Lake County Visitors Bureau; (440) 975-1234; mylakeoh.com
Hiking groups: Cleveland Hiking Club; clevelandhikingclub.org
Northeast Ohio Hiking Club; meetup.com/NEOHiking/
Lake County YMCA Walking/Running Club; lakecountyymca.org/programs/running-walking-club
Camping: Penitentiary Glen Reservation has a reservable campsite; learn more at lake metroparks.com/register-reserve/reserve-a-shelter/tent-camping/penitentiary-glen -reservation-campsite/, or call (440) 256-1404.

17 Chair Factory Falls

Jordan Creek was once home to a waterwheel that powered a chair factory, hence the name Chair Factory Falls. As is the case with many waterfall hikes in northeast Ohio, what was once a location of industry is now a place of beauty and recreation. Follow the Greenway Corridor—a rail trail that once carried B&O Railroad tracks—to a footpath built by Lake Metroparks to the tall, cascading waterfall situated in a forested setting.

Height of falls: 35 feet tall, up to 50 feet wide
Type of falls: Cascade
Distance: 1.8 miles out and back
Difficulty: Easy
Hiking time: About 45 minutes to 1 hour
Trail names: Buckeye Trail/Jordan Creek Crossing Trail, Greenway Corridor, Chair Factory Falls Trail
Trail surface: Dirt, asphalt, gravel
Seasons and hours: Best in spring or fall after rain; open daily, 6 a.m. to 11 p.m.
Canine compatibility: Leashed dogs permitted

Trailhead facilities: None; the Environmental Learning Center with restrooms and water is nearby.
Trail contact: Lake Metroparks Jordan Creek Park; (440) 256-2118; lakemetroparks.com/parks-trails/jordan-creek-park
  Jordan Creek Park's Environmental Learning Center has educational programs and also is rentable as a venue; (440) 348-7275; lakemetroparks.com/parks-trails/jordan-creek-park/environmental-learning-center. It's open Mon through Fri, 9 a.m. to 5 p.m., when a staff person is present; closed to the public when rented.

Finding the trailhead: From I-90 east of Cleveland, take exit 200 for SR 44 South to the first light at Auburn Road. Turn left and then take an immediate left and continue 0.2 mile to Concord Hambden Road. Turn right and go 1.4 miles to Alexander Road. Turn left and then left again at the park entrance, marked with a large sign. In about 100 yards, arrive at the first parking pullout on the right, marked with a sign for the Buckeye Trail and other trails. GPS: N42 40.28' / W81 12.58'

The Hike

This is a waterfall hike that's great for the whole family, with much to do in addition to the hike to Chair Factory Falls. There is an environmental learning center with educational displays, a nature play area complete with a children's climbing wall and ziplines, plus ADA-accessible features in the park for anyone in your party who may need features that are wheelchair accessible.

Start at the trailhead closest to the park entrance in order to add a second waterfall to your hike. You will begin on the statewide, 1,400-mile Buckeye Trail. Follow the blue blazes for the first portion of the hike. Immediately walk down to Jordan Creek. The described hike turns left before the creek, but make a short side trip to the footbridge that crosses the creek and look upstream. Here you'll see your first waterfall of the hike. It's a small unnamed cascade, but quite attractive nonetheless.

Chair Factory Falls

Walk a shaded footpath until you get to the paved Greenway Corridor. This is a rail trail that once carried tracks of the Baltimore & Ohio Railroad. This is an asphalt trail and not well shaded, so it's best to avoid in the midday heat of summer. Then exit the bike path to take the Chair Factory Falls Trail to the waterfall. Although you can hear the traffic from I-90 on this portion of trail, it otherwise has a calming, deep woods feel. Walk under the shade of oak, hickory, and maple trees—then hemlock trees as you walk down into the gorge.

Chair Factory Falls is substantial, particularly after a recent rain. In the nineteenth century this was the site of a sawmill and chair factory. Pack a lunch and plan to spend some time here; there are benches and interpretive signs near the falls.

Miles and Directions

0.0 Start on the Buckeye Trail at the right (east) edge of the parking pullout. Following the blue blazes, walk down toward the creek for about 150 feet. From here, the BT turns left onto a crushed gravel path. (**Option:** It's worth first walking to the bridge and looking upstream for a small cascade.)

0.1 Ascend out of the valley by way of wooden stairs. At the top of the stairs, there is a fork. Take the left fork, staying on the BT.

0.2 Cross the park road. The crushed gravel path turns to asphalt. Come to a junction with a spur to the trailhead from the main parking lot. Continue straight.

0.3 Arrive at a T intersection with the paved Greenway Corridor. Turn right. You will pass a couple of access trails on the left. Continue straight.

0.6 At a sign for Chair Factory Falls, turn right off the pavement and hike a gravel path.

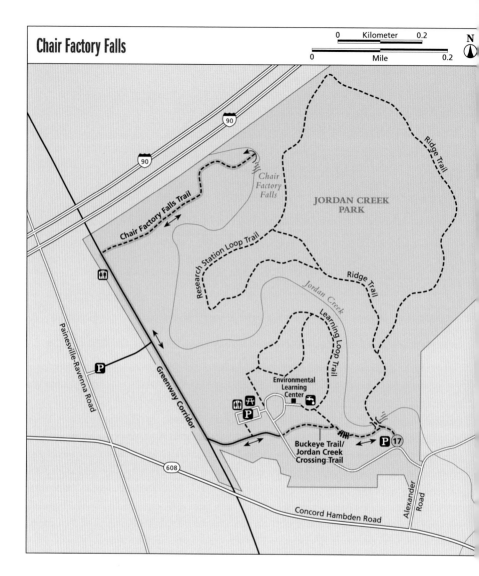

0.9 The path descends into the valley and ends at an overlook for the falls. From here, retrace your steps to the trailhead.

1.8 Arrive back at the trailhead.

Hike Information

Local information: Lake County Visitors Bureau; (440) 975-1234; mylakeoh.com
Organizations: Buckeye Trail Association; (740) 394-2008; buckeyetrail.org
Hiking groups: Cleveland Hiking Club; clevelandhikingclub.org
Northeast Ohio Hiking Club; meetup.com/NEOHiking/
Lake County YMCA Walking/Running Club; lakecountyymca.org/programs/running-walking-club

18 Hell Hollow Waterfalls

If you're not afraid of hiking the 262 stairs down into and then back again out of Hell Hollow, this is actually hiking heaven. Once in the valley, you're rewarded with the freedom to wade in Paine Creek. There are four small waterfalls on Paine Creek and its tributaries within the park—more ephemeral falls when it's been raining—so plan enough time to explore. A couple of the falls are visible from the end of the formal trail if you're feeling less adventurous.

Height of falls: Varies; most are only a few feet tall but span the width of the creek, which is up to 45 feet
Type of falls: Shelf, tier, cascade
Distance: 0.9-mile reverse lollipop
Difficulty: Moderate due to steep ascent out of gorge
Hiking time: About 30 minutes
Trail names: Beech Ridge Loop Trail, Wildcat Trail

Trail surface: Dirt
Seasons and hours: Best in late spring and early summer; open daily, 6 a.m. to 11 p.m.
Canine compatibility: Leashed dogs permitted
Trailhead facilities: Vault toilet
Trail contact: Lake Metroparks Hell Hollow Wilderness Area; (440) 358-7275; lakemetro parks.com/parks-trails/hell-hollow-wilderness -area

Finding the trailhead: From I-90 east of Cleveland, take exit 205 and head east on SR 86 for 4.9 miles to Thompson Road (you will drive through a roundabout along the way). Turn left onto Thompson Road and go 2.2 miles to Leroy Center Road. Turn left and drive 0.9 mile to the park entrance on the right (Leroy Center goes from gravel to paved then back to gravel). Turn right into the park entrance and drive 0.1 mile to the parking lot. The trail starts from the parking lot. Take the gravel path toward the kiosk and the vault toilet. GPS: N41 41.21' / W81 07.01'

The Hike

Hell Hollow Wilderness Area's 100-foot-deep ravine was created when the last glacier retreated some 12,000 years ago as Paine Creek carved into the surrounding Chagrin Shale. Today Paine Creek is home to multiple waterfalls, including the famous Paine Falls. Paine Falls is in a separate park and does not require a hike but is well worth a visit while you're in the area. The two-tiered cascade is some 30 feet high and 80 feet wide.

The hike at Hell Hollow begins at the top of the gorge. It's the heart-pounding ascent back out of the gorge that gives it the name Hell Hollow. Walk the Beech Ridge Loop Trail where, yes, you will find a maple-beech forest abutting a wet flat-woods ecosystem. Look also for huge oak trees—and for the "dinosaur toes" that the large oak roots protrude into the trail. Additionally, listen and look for woodpeckers, warblers, and many other birds; Audubon Ohio has named this an Important Bird Area. In the spring, look for wildflowers like jack-in-the-pulpit and wild geranium.

A shelf waterfall in Hell Hollow Wilderness Area

After taking the Wildcat Trail to descend the steep stairs into the ravine, arrive at Paine Creek, where you will encounter a northern hardwood-hemlock forest. The rocky beach here makes for perfect rock skipping. In front of you is the confluence with a tributary to Paine Creek and a small, tiered waterfall. Upstream on Paine Creek is another small shelf waterfall that spans the width of the creek, which is usually at least 20 feet wide. Know that flow can be quite low, however, so a visit in spring or after a rain is essential to take in any substantial waterfalls.

Best of all, off-trail hiking/wading in the creek is permitted here. Take time to explore Paine Creek and its tributaries. There are at least four waterfalls in the park, and even where the water isn't falling, it is riffling. Enjoy this beautiful creek, and take the necessary precautions to avoid getting washed away or experiencing hypothermia. One more bonus: There is a campsite here; contact Lake Metroparks to reserve it.

Miles and Directions

0.0 Start on the gravel path on the far (west) end of the parking lot. Walk between the vault toilet and the kiosk. This is the Beech Ridge Loop Trail.

0.2 Arrive at a three-way junction; go straight. This begins the out-and-back Wildcat Trail that takes you down to Paine Creek.

0.4 After descending the stairs, come to Paine Creek. There are small waterfalls on the creek and at the confluence with a tributary. After exploring, turn around and walk back up the stairs.

0.6 Return to the junction with the Beech Ridge Loop Trail. Turn left.

0.9 Pass the shelter house and arrive back at the parking lot near the trailhead.

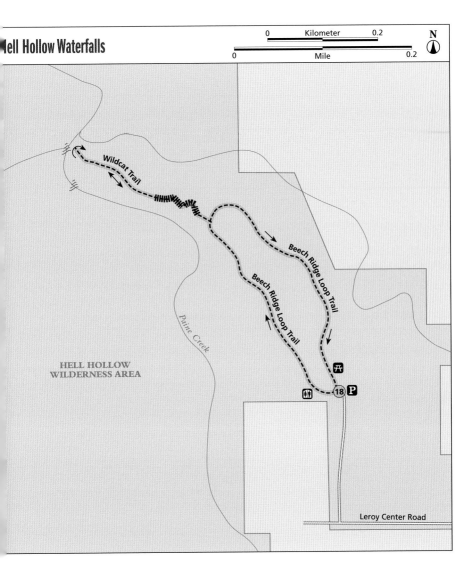

Wildcat Trail

Beech Ridge Loop Trail

Beech Ridge Loop Trail

Paine Creek

HELL HOLLOW
WILDERNESS AREA

18 P

Leroy Center Road

Hike Information

Local information: Lake County Visitors Bureau; (440) 975-1234; mylakeoh.com

Hiking groups: Cleveland Hiking Club; clevelandhikingclub.org

Northeast Ohio Hiking Club; meetup.com/NEOHiking/

Lake County YMCA Walking/Running Club; lakecountyymca.org/programs/running-walking-club

Camping: An on-site campsite is available by reservation. Info and online reservations are available at lakemetroparks.com/register-reserve/reserve-a-shelter/tent-camping/hell-hollow-wilderness-area-campsite/, or call (440) 358-7275.

19 Mill Creek Falls, Hogback Ridge Park

The Grand River is a state-designated Wild and Scenic River. And its tributary, Mill Creek? Even prettier. Come to Hogback Ridge Park in the spring for a hike along the creek past cascades, drops, and swirls. Or, heck, hike in the creek for that matter—wading is allowed. Add outstanding spring wildflowers, and—if you plan ahead—stay overnight in an on-site cabin.

Height of falls: Varies; up to 8 feet tall and 80 feet wide
Type of falls: Cascade, plunge
Distance: 1.6-mile lollipop
Difficulty: Moderate due to steep gorge access
Hiking time: About 45 minutes
Trail names: Hemlock Ridge Loop Trail, Bluebell Valley Path, Meadow Rim Trail

Trail surface: Dirt, gravel, boardwalk
Seasons and hours: Best in Apr; open daily, 6 a.m. to 11 p.m.
Canine compatibility: Leashed dogs permitted
Trailhead facilities: Vault toilet, picnic area
Trail contact: Lake Metroparks Hogback Ridge Park; (440) 358-7275; lakemetroparks.com/parks-trails/hogback-ridge-park

Finding the trailhead: From I-90 east of Cleveland, take exit 212 and go south on SR 528 for 1.6 miles to Griswold Road. Turn left and go 0.9 mile to Emerson Road. Turn left and go 0.5 mile into the park/parking lot. The Hemlock Ridge Loop Trail begins next to the vault toilet. GPS: N41 44.38' / W81 01.50'

The Hike

Prepare to be delighted on a hike along Mill Creek. Part of the delight is that you can hike *in* Mill Creek. Wading is allowed, so enjoy rock skipping, midstream photography, wildlife viewing, and all sorts of other discoveries that "creeking" allows.

Begin at the picnic area along Emerson Road (the Emerson family operated a mill near the confluence of Mill Creek and the Grand River). From here, take a wide gravel trail to a 1,300-foot-long boardwalk, which is ADA accessible. From the boardwalk, descend stairs into Mill Creek Valley on the Bluebell Valley Path—if you come in late April, you'll learn why the trail is so named. The forest floor is covered in Virginia bluebells plus ramps (wild leeks), trillium, trout lily, and other choice spring wildflowers.

Arrive at Mill Creek, where you are immediately greeted with a shallow, cascading waterfall rushing over the shale bedrock. On the other side of the creek is the namesake Hogback Ridge, which separates Mill Creek from the Grand River at this point, but they converge downstream from here. The shale bluffs here are signature of the rivers along Steelhead Alley, the streams that feed into the eastern basin of Lake Erie, and are home to steelhead trout. Look for fly fishers fall through spring here. And look for avian fishers—great blue herons—year-round.

A waterfall along Mill Creek in Hogback Ridge Park

Continue your hike upstream. Listen for birds and frogs, and keep a constant eye on Mill Creek. Multiple river-wide cascading waterfalls, water swirls, and small plunges exist all along this section of the creek. While none are massive cataracts, the quantity and variety of falls here are not an everyday occurrence elsewhere in the state.

All told, there are more than 5 miles of trails in this park, which is mostly wooded with a maple-beech forest, with plenty of sycamores and hemlocks in the cool, wet riparian areas. There is a single cabin, the Strong Cabin, available for rent on the property. Call the park district to book it in advance (see "Trail contact" above).

Miles and Directions

0.0 Start in front of the vault toilet, where you'll see a post with a blaze for the Hemlock Ridge Loop Trail: white hemlock needles on a gold background. Walk around the right of the toilet and past a junction with the Meadow Rim Trail on the right, continuing straight. At a junction with the boardwalk, continue straight, following the blaze.

0.2 Pass a second junction with the Meadow Rim Trail on the right. Continue straight, staying on the boardwalk.

0.3 Come to a junction with the Bluebell Valley Path; the blaze is a white bluebell flower on a blue background. Turn right and descend the stairs to the valley. Arrive at the banks of Mill Creek, where you will see the first of a series of cascades. Turn right and parallel the creek while walking upstream, passing several cascades and falls.

1.0 The trail ascends out of the valley, still paralleling the stream at first.

1.3 At the top of the ridge, come to a T intersection with the Meadow Rim Trail, marked with a white butterfly on a pink background. Turn right.

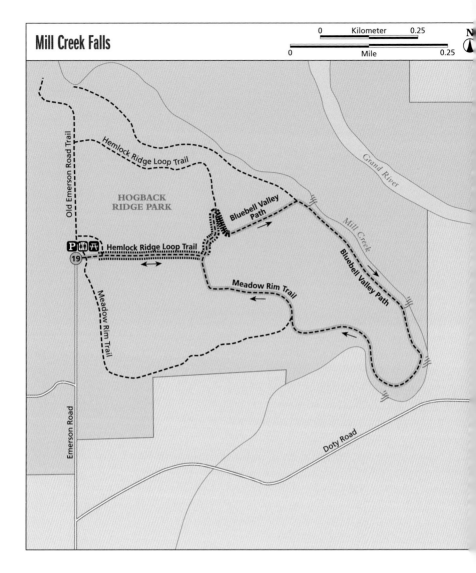

0   Kilometer   0.25

0   Mile   0.25

N

Old Emerson Road Trail

Hemlock Ridge Loop Trail

HOGBACK
RIDGE PARK

Bluebell Valley Path

Grand River

Mill Creek

Hemlock Ridge Loop Trail

19

Meadow Rim Trail

Bluebell Valley Path

Meadow Rim Trail

Emerson Road

Doty Road

1.5   Return to a junction from the beginning of the hike, where the Meadow Rim Trail meets the Hemlock Ridge Loop Trail at the boardwalk. Turn left and retrace your steps to the trailhead.

1.6   Arrive back at the trailhead.

Hike Information

Local information: Lake County Visitors Bureau; (440) 975-1234; mylakeoh.com

Hiking groups: Cleveland Hiking Club; clevelandhikingclub.org

Northeast Ohio Hiking Club; meetup.com/NEOHiking/

Lake County YMCA Walking/Running Club; lakecountyymca.org/programs/running-walking-club

20 Cascade and Minnehaha Falls

It's right there in the name—the Sharon Conglomerate ledges that can top 40 feet are what Nelson-Kennedy Ledges State Park is known for. This small but magical park is full of nooks and crannies and cool rock hallways to explore. The ledges act as nurseries to the hemlock and beech trees whose roots grow over the rock, in turn providing a home to ferns and wildflowers. And of course there are the waterfalls. Hike to the 35-foot-tall Cascade Falls and then the two-part Minnehaha Falls.

Height of falls: 35 feet; 18 feet
Type of falls: Cascade; plunge
Distance: 1.8-mile trail system
Difficulty: Moderate due to some steep or slick terrain and tight squeezes
Hiking time: About 1 hour
Trail names: Yellow Trail, White Trail, Red Trail, Blue Trail
Trail surface: Dirt, rock

Seasons and hours: Good year-round after rain; open daily, half hour before sunrise to half hour after sunset
Canine compatibility: Leashed dogs permitted
Trailhead facilities: Vault toilet, picnic area
Trail contact: Nelson-Kennedy Ledges State Park; (330) 235-0030; ohiodnr.gov/go-and-do/plan-a-visit/find-a-property/nelson kennedy-ledges-state-park

Finding the trailhead: From the junction of US 422 and SR 282 in Garrettsville, go south 1.7 miles to the Nelson-Kennedy Ledges parking lot on the left. GPS: N41 19.43' / W81 02.21'

The Hike

Geology is on full display at Nelson-Kennedy Ledges. You can understand the process that creates sedimentary rock here. It's easy to see how ancient streams deposited and layered sand over and over. These streams also carried rounded quartzite pebbles that ended up in the sand. Time, pressure, and temperature created today's Sharon Conglomerate sandstone. Add waterfalls pouring over these rocks and you've got a great waterfall hike.

This is a beautiful and easy hike to the waterfalls through rocky cliffs, hallways, and squeezes. Overuse and carelessness have created a spiderweb of trails everywhere, but keep an eye out for blazes and you should be able to avoid getting lost. You're never far from earshot of the road. Also pay close attention to property boundaries in this small park so that you do not veer onto private property.

The hike rewards you with an almost immediate view of Cascade Falls. Begin among the slump blocks and ledges. Walk through a forest of hemlock, beech, and maple while winding around the many rock faces. Under Cascade Falls is Gold Hunter's Cave, which got its name during a gold rush of sorts around 1870. But as it turns out, the gold diggers who came here found only fool's gold.

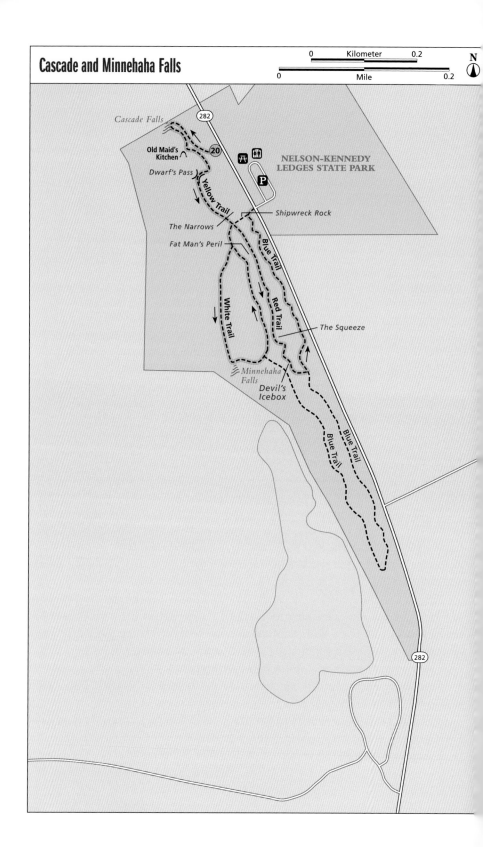

Cascade and Minnehaha Falls

0   Kilometer   0.2

0   Mile   0.2

N

Cascade Falls

282

20

Old Maid's Kitchen

Dwarf's Pass

Yellow Trail

NELSON-KENNEDY LEDGES STATE PARK

P

Shipwreck Rock

The Narrows

Fat Man's Peril

Blue Trail

Red Trail

White Trail

The Squeeze

Minnehaha Falls

Devil's Icebox

Blue Trail

Blue Trail

282

Cascade Falls

Reverse direction and walk through a dark cave named Old Maid's Kitchen. Work your way out of the cave then, shortly down the trail, do a limbo move to pass under the aptly named Dwarf's Pass. In springtime these cool recesses are home to abundant wildflowers, including red trillium, spring beauty, Solomon's seal, and hepatica. A multitude of ferns grow out of the rocky soil, even directly out of the rocks themselves. Look for the common wood, Christmas, and maidenhair ferns.

The trail soon reaches the top of the ledges and continues through a mature maple-beech forest. From this vantage you can look down on the two-part Minnehaha Falls and into the slot canyon the falls have created. The falls are about 18 feet high; the lower section is essentially a set of rapids cutting through the rock. Cliffs are as high as 40 feet, so exercise caution, especially if you're hiking with children or pets. This portion of the trail loops back and returns to the bottom of the ledges, where the passageways narrow considerably. In winter, ice builds up quickly, so spikes for your boots are a good idea.

The next part of the path has a couple of very small squeezes that aren't even big enough for both you and your day pack. After wiggling through these tight spots—with names like Fat Man's Peril and The Squeeze—enjoy the cool damp and the acoustics of Devil's Icebox. From here return farther downslope into a cool weather–loving forest that includes hemlock, Canada yew, and yellow birch. End the hike at the southern trailhead next to the parking lot.

Miles and Directions

0.0 Start from the northern trailhead, across the road from the picnic area. Facing the trail-head bulletin board, take off to the right and follow the yellow-blazed Yellow Trail along the ledges to Cascade Falls. Pass a box canyon on the left.

0.1 The trail leads to Cascade Falls. After viewing the falls, retrace your steps to the box can-yon. Turn right, staying near the rocks and ascending slightly. Then walk into the Old Maid's Kitchen cave.

0.2 Exit the cave to the left, just past the boardwalk. Outside the cave, turn right. At the end of the rock face to your right, turn right again into the rocks and then follow another boardwalk through Dwarf's Pass. After crossing a second boardwalk, continue straight and ascend out of the cool rock shelters.

0.4 Walk atop the rocks to a four-way intersection. Turn right onto the White Trail, following the white blazes.

0.7 Before reaching a chain-link fence, the trail curves to the left, overlooking some nice views from the top of the rocks, including Minnehaha Falls.

0.8 A wooden footbridge to the right allows you to peer into the mini slot canyons below. Walk to the footbridge then turn back, looking for the white blazes.

1.0 Arrive back at the four-way intersection. Turn right and walk about 100 feet. To the left is a metal yellow hiker blaze. Across from this blaze, look for a narrow squeeze between two rocks, marked with a faint red blaze. Walk through this opening. You are now on the Red Trail.

1.2 About 50 feet past another narrow squeeze, come to a fork. Turn right and head upward. At the top of the rocks, there's a red-blazed beech tree. Just past the beech tree, descend into the gorge again. (*Note:* Be careful here; it's an especially slick spot when wet.)

1.3 Come out of the last squeeze and look left for a blaze. Beyond that, a double blaze indi-cates a turn to the right to join the Blue Trail.

1.4 Arrive at Devil's Icebox. After exploring, walk downstream toward a footbridge. Instead of crossing the footbridge, turn left and walk north for the return trip, following the blue blazes for the Blue Trail.

1.8 Come to a T intersection. Turn right and walk toward the road to arrive at the southern trailhead, across from the parking lot. Follow the road north to arrive back at the trailhead by the parking lot entrance.

Hike Information

Local information: Central Portage County Visitor and Convention Bureau; (800) 764-8768

Organizations: Friends of Punderson exists to benefit Punderson State Park as well as other parks in the region, including Nelson-Kennedy Ledges; friendsofpunderson .com

Hiking groups: Cleveland Hiking Club; clevelandhikingclub.org

Northeast Ohio Hiking Club; meetup.com/NEOHiking/

Camping: The adjacent Nelson Ledges Quarry Park has camping; (440) 548-2716; nlqp.com. Check the schedule, as the park also hosts music festivals.

21 Lanterman's Falls

Lanterman's Falls is one of the most Instagram-worthy waterfalls in the state. But put down the phone and get up close and personal with the waterfall, the surrounding trails, and the restored Lanterman's Mill, which is a working mill. Think of it as a flower-meets-flour hike: After taking in the wildflowers along Mill Creek, allot a few minutes to stop in and view the inner workings of the mill.

Height of falls: 22 feet
Type of falls: Tiered
Distance: 1.8-mile loop
Difficulty: Easy
Hiking time: About 1 hour
Trail names: East Gorge Trail, West Gorge Trail
Trail surface: Dirt, boardwalk, grass, pavement
Seasons and hours: Good year-round; open daily, sunrise to sunset

Canine compatibility: Leashed dogs permitted
Trailhead facilities: Seasonal restrooms and water
Trail contact: Mill Creek Park; (330) 740-7115; millcreekmetroparks.org/visit/places/mill-creek-park/lantermans-mill/
Special considerations: Parking is somewhat limited; try to visit on a weekday, or arrive early or late in the day on weekends.

Finding the trailhead: From I-80 on the northwest side of Youngstown, exit south onto SR 46. Travel 5.5 miles and turn left (east) onto US 62. Travel 4.9 miles; cross over Mill Creek and, just on the other side, turn left into the parking lot. From the parking lot, walk upstream on a paved path, crossing over US 62 at a crosswalk, and then to Lanterman's Mill. The trail starts in front of the mill. GPS: N40 13.22' / W81 48.64'

The Hike

Lanterman's Falls is a natural 23-foot drop along the aptly named Mill Creek. This was an obvious place to build a mill, and German Lanterman did so in 1845–46. The mill was restored in 1985, and milling began again. Before or after your hike, it's worth going into the mill to see its inner workings. There is a nominal entry fee, and the mill sells stone-ground cornmeal, buckwheat, and whole wheat.

Beginning from the mill, hike downstream on the East Gorge Trail, parallel to Mill Creek. Enjoy walking in a cozy gorge with the creek to your left. Hemlock trees, which prefer cool and damp conditions, thrive here. Look and listen for water-loving birds like belted kingfishers. Because it's cool and damp, come prepared. Waterproof shoes for mud (or microspikes for ice in winter) are recommended.

The trail eventually leaves the edge of the creek, crosses Valley Drive, and then crosses a field and passes a picnic area before you walk across the creek on the sidewalk of a silver suspension bridge. After crossing the suspension bridge, pick up the West Gorge Trail. (**Option:** Add another 3.0-mile loop by walking the West Cohasset Trail, which begins here, to the East Cohasset Trail. This will take you past some additional water features.)

Lanterman's Falls and Lanterman's Mill

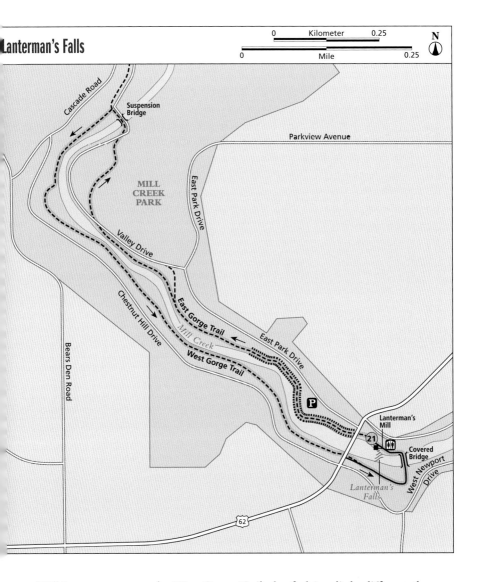

Walking upstream on the West Gorge Trail, the feel is a little different than on the east side of Mill Creek. Rock outcroppings hem you in. In the spring, look for a big patch of skunk cabbage in a broad marshy area. Other spring wildflowers include trout lily, mayapple, and flowering redbud trees. Walk under a rock shelter before ascending out of the creek valley among large oak and beech trees.

The trail goes under the US 62 bridge (the best place to photograph the falls is from the sidewalk on this bridge) and then joins a park road. Follow the road downhill to the covered bridge. The covered bridge, completed in 1989, is designed after the original bridge from the 1800s that farmers used when they brought grain to the mill. After crossing over Mill Creek on the covered bridge, return to the mill where you began.

Miles and Directions

0.0 Start by Lanterman's Mill at the trailhead marked with a sign for the East Gorge Trail. Walk downstream, under the US 62 bridge, and onto a boardwalk.

0.4 The trail forks; take the left fork, staying by the creek.

0.6 The East Gorge Trail ends. Cross the road and walk across the field, toward the picnic area. Before the picnic area, trend left toward the silver bridge and walk through a gap in the fence. Walk over the bridge. (**Option:** You can also follow the creek to the bridge.)

0.8 On the other side of Mill Creek, turn left and walk upstream on the West Gorge Trail, marked with a sign.

1.6 After walking under a rock shelter and ascending out of the valley, come to a fork. Take the left fork and hike under the US 62 bridge.

1.7 Join the paved service road and continue walking upstream (downhill) toward the covered bridge.

1.75 At a bend in the road, another trail leaves the pavement; stay on the pavement and then walk across the covered bridge.

1.8 Arrive back at Lanterman's Mill.

Hike Information

Local information: Youngstown Live/Mahoning County Convention and Visitors Bureau; (800) 447-8201; youngstownlive.com

Lanterman's Mill is open May through Oct, Tues through Sun, 10 a.m. to 5 p.m.; closed holidays. See "Trail contact" above for contact information.

Organizations: Mill Creek MetroParks Foundation; lovemillcreek.org

Hiking groups: Cleveland Hiking Club; clevelandhikingclub.org

Northeast Ohio Hiking Club; meetup.com/NEOHiking/

22 Fleming Falls

As of 2022, you can find out for yourself what the campers at the old Camp Mowana knew for decades: that this 183-acre property is home to several seasonal waterfalls, including the 15-foot plunge known as Fleming Falls. Hats off to Richland County Parks for purchasing this property and opening it to the public. You can now take a diverse hike past a handful of waterfalls, through a pine forest, and through a wildflower meadow.

Height of falls: About 15 feet
Type of falls: Plunge
Distance: 1.8-mile loop
Difficulty: Easy
Hiking time: About 1 hour
Trail names: Pine Woods Paths, Barn View Meadows, South Fork Loop, connector paths
Trail surface: Dirt, gravel
Seasons and hours: Best in spring; open weekends, dawn to dusk
Canine compatibility: Leashed dogs permitted; you must pick up after your pet.
Trailhead facilities: Porta potty

Trail contact: Fleming Falls Preserve; (419) 884-FROG (419-884-3764); richlandcounty parks.com
Gorman Nature Center; (419) 884-3764; richlandcountyoh.gov/maps/location/Richland CountyGormanNatureCenter
Special considerations: Fleming Falls Preserve is a work in progress; check the park's Facebook page to keep up to date on site development and hours of operation. The plan is to be open year-round in the future. There are no trash cans, so pack it in, pack it out.

Finding the trailhead: From I-71 exit 176 near Mansfield, go west on Crider Road 0.2 mile to Bowen Road. Turn right and go 1 mile to Fleming Falls Road. Turn left and continue 0.7 mile to the entrance on the left at a gap in a split-rail fence. The trailhead kiosk is on the western edge of the parking lot. N40 47.49' / W82 25.50'

The Hike

Get in touch with your inner summer-camp kid at Fleming Falls Park and Preserve. After seventy-eight years as a Lutheran camp, the former Camp Mowana had its final season in 2019, and the property is still full of summer church camp artifacts: cabins, an outdoor chapel, an education building, and more. Even better, it's home to a dozen waterfalls, some of which are ephemeral.

Begin by hiking down to the confluence of Fleming Creek and its south fork. Immediately you'll see small cascades. In less than 0.5 mile, you'll come to Fleming Falls, the largest waterfall in the park. After checking out the falls from the falls overlook platform, walk through an aromatic white pine forest on a blanket of pine needles. Then hike through a short section of meadow—in summer look for black raspberries and flowers like milkweed; in the fall look for goldenrod and aster.

Fleming Falls

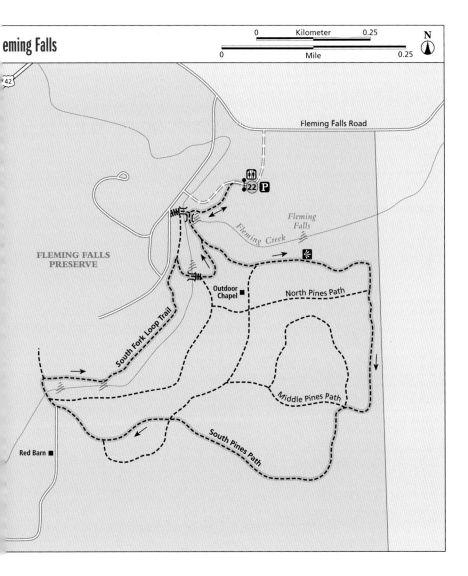

Between the forest and fields, this is a good birding destination. Look and listen for blue jays, cedar waxwings, and juncos.

The final portion of the hike follows the South Fork of Fleming Creek downstream on the blue-blazed South Fork Loop. Look for a series of small waterfalls all along this creek, especially after a rainfall. You'll continue to see old summer camp cabins along this stretch. The western part of the preserve has some more meadow trails and a small pond. Be sure to check the park district's Facebook page before your hike, as this preserve is still a work in progress.

Miles and Directions

0.0 Start at the trailhead kiosk at the parking lot. Walk down the gravel road into the woods. In about 500 feet, before you cross a bridge, turn left and cross the grass down to the trail by a split-rail fence.

0.1 Arrive at a footbridge over a confluence of two creeks. Walk the L-shaped footbridge across both creeks and start ascending out of the creek valley, following a sign for the falls overlook.

0.2 The trail forks. Take the left fork, up the steps, toward the falls overlook.

0.3 Pass the outdoor chapel on the right and come to a junction. Trend left, following the sign for the falls overlook.

0.4 Arrive at the overlook for Fleming Falls. Continue straight. The trail trends to the right (south).

0.5 Come to a junction with the North Pines Path on the right. Continue straight.

0.7 Arrive at a four-way junction. Turn left onto the South Pines Path.

1.0 Come to a junction and continue straight, walking into the meadow. In about 100 feet, come to a four-way junction. Continue straight, toward the red barn.

1.1 At another junction, continue straight toward the red barn.

1.2 Come to a staggered junction with a gravel doubletrack. Turn left; in about 40 feet, turn right and cross the stream on an old road.

1.25 After crossing the stream, come to a staggered five-way junction. Turn right, entering the forest on the blue-blazed South Fork Loop Trail.

1.5 Reach a four-way junction. Turn right and cross the stream on a footbridge near a small waterfall. Then take the stairs out of the valley.

1.6 Come to a fork. Take the left fork and arrive at the first junction you came to at the beginning of the hike. Turn left and retrace your steps to the trailhead.

1.8 Arrive back at the trailhead.

Hike Information

Local information: Destination Mansfield-Richland County; (419) 525-1300; destinationmansfield.com

Organizations: Friends of Richland County Park District; (419) 884-3764; sites.google.com/view/friendsofrichlandcountyparks

Camping: Charles Mill Lake Park; (419) 368-6885; charlesmillpark.mwcd.org

23 Hemlock Falls

True to its name, the tiered Hemlock Falls crashes down a sandstone cliff where it is surrounded by evergreen hemlock trees. From Native tribes to early European settlers to today's hikers, Hemlock Falls has long been a place of beauty and gathering for locals and travelers alike. Thanks to collaboration between local landowners, the park district, and conservationists, Hemlock Falls is open to the public and the site's infrastructure is good for a nice hike to the falls.

Height of falls: About 45 feet
Type of falls: Tiered
Distance: 2.2 miles out and back
Difficulty: Easy
Hiking time: About 1 hour
Trail names: Main Trail, Hemlock Falls Spur
Trail surface: Dirt, grass

Seasons and hours: Best in spring; open daily, sunrise to dark
Canine compatibility: Leashed dogs permitted
Trailhead facilities: None
Trail contact: North Central Ohio Land Conservancy; (419) 522-6262; ncolc.org

Finding the trailhead: From I-71 exit 165 south of Mansfield, take SR 97 for 12.5 miles to Bunker Hill Road (watch for turns on SR 97). Turn left onto Bunker Hill Road and continue 0.8 mile to Tugend Road (you'll see a large "Camp Otyokwah" sign). Turn left and go 0.1 mile to a small gravel parking lot on the right. GPS: N40 36.18' / W82 22.51'

The Hike

Historical records and photographs show people gathering at Hemlock Falls for many generations. For quite a while in recent history, the falls were not open to the public. But then the North Central Ohio Land Conservancy stepped in to work with the Richland County Park District and another landowner, Camp Nuhop, to create public access to the falls. Many know this area as the onetime home of the Mohican Outdoor School.

Begin at a small gravel parking lot between Tugend Road and the Tugend Prairie. In summer and fall, this tallgrass prairie includes flowering plants like butterfly weed (yes, look for butterflies), bergamot, wild sunflower, wingstem, goldenrod, and ironweed. Look for the bluebirds that have taken up residence in the bluebird boxes. Other common bird species seen here are wrens, swallows, flycatchers, woodpeckers, and hummingbirds.

Start on the Main Trail. The entire trail system is consistently blazed with brown posts; keep an eye out for the next post and you won't get lost. Walk along the edge of the prairie and a tree line until you enter the forest. This section of forest is quite young due to logging, and the understory is choked with multiflora rose. Walk through the woods on a mowed grass path. After crossing Bunker Hill Road, the

Hemlock Falls

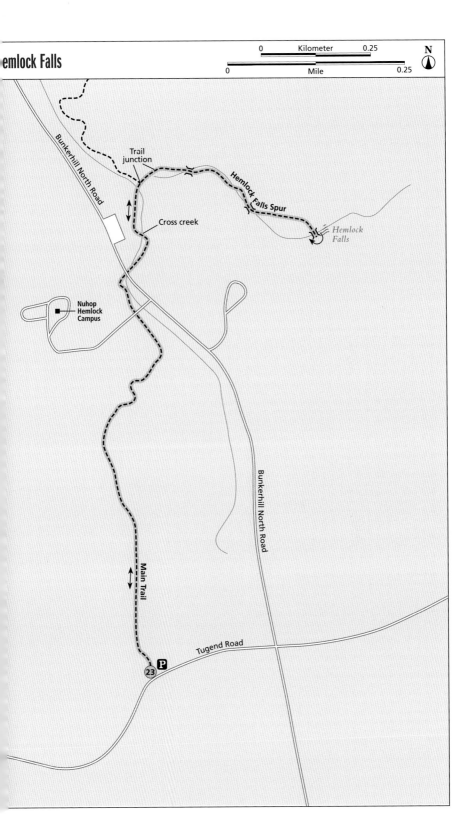

emlock Falls

0   Kilometer   0.25

0   Mile   0.25

N

Bunkerhill North Road

Trail junction

Hemlock Falls Spur

Hemlock Falls

Cross creek

Nuhop Hemlock Campus

Bunkerhill North Road

Main Trail

Tugend Road

P

23

nature of the forest changes, with more mature maple, buckeye, and pine trees. As you approach the falls, spring wildflowers become dense, including spring beauty, blood-root, and Dutchman's breeches.

Turn off the Main Trail onto the Hemlock Falls Spur; soon you will likely hear the falls before you see them. Approach along Hemlock Run and view the falls from a footbridge, where the trail ends. Hemlock Falls crashes down a sandstone cliff line, and then Hemlock Run flows right under your feet on its downstream course to the Clear Fork of the Mohican River. Contact NCOLC about getting a permit to continue hiking beyond this point, where you can glimpse the intermittent Horseshoe Falls when it's flowing.

If you have the time, be sure to return to the Main Trail from the Hemlock Falls Spur and continue hiking north. Further exploration in this direction will take you to a more mature forest, to the top of Eagle's Nest Rock, and to another prairie full of cup plant, wingstem, dogbane, and more, plus prairie birds like bluebirds. You'll also see the result of the tornado that blew through here in 2022; the trail has been rerouted and reopened, but a lot of large downed trees have opened up the canopy significantly.

Miles and Directions

0.0 Start from the gravel parking lot between Tugend Road and Tugend Prairie. Walk uphill toward the prairie and trend left, looking for a "Main Trail" sign. Turn right at the sign and follow an old lane along a tree line.

0.2 Come to a fork and take the left fork.

0.3 Arrive at an open field with a gas well. Trend right.

0.5 Cross the gravel driveway to Camp Nuhop.

0.6 Cross Bunker Hill Road.

0.7 Cross the creek.

0.8 Come to a T intersection. You'll see a gravel parking lot on the left. Turn right and almost immediately arrive at a four-way junction. Turn right and take the trail marked for Hemlock Falls. In about 100 feet, the trail forks; take the right fork.

1.1 End at a footbridge below the falls. Retrace your steps to the trailhead.

2.2 Arrive back at the trailhead.

Hike Information

Local information: Destination Mansfield-Richland County; (419) 525-1300; destinationmansfield.com

Discover Mohican/Mohican-Loudonville Visitors Bureau; discovermohican.com

Organizations: Mohican Trails Club; mohicantrailsclub.org; twitter.com/mohicanc

Camping: Malabar Farm State Park Campground; (866) 644-6727; ohiodnr.gov/go -and-do/plan-a-visit/find-a-property/malabar-farm-state-park-campground

Mohican State Park Campground; (866) 644-6727; ohiodnr.gov/go-and-do/plan-a -visit/find-a-property/mohican-state-park-campground

24 Big and Little Lyons Falls

Come for the waterfalls and stay for the weekend. Mohican State Park is full of water-based fun: waterfalls, tubing, canoeing, fly fishing. And then there's camping, backpacking, and mountain biking. Start your weekend with the Lyons Falls Trail that takes you to Big Lyons Falls and Little Lyons Falls—the first an 80-foot plunge over a recess cave followed by another 25-foot waterfall pouring into a tight gorge. Along the way, parallel the shaded, riffling Clear Fork of the Mohican River.

Height of falls: 80 feet; 25 feet

Type of falls: Cave; plunge

Distance: 2.5-mile lollipop

Difficulty: Moderate due to elevation gain and stream crossings

Hiking time: About 1 hour

Trail name: Lyons Falls Trail

Trail surface: Dirt with some boardwalk sections

Seasons and hours: Best in late winter and early spring; open daily, half hour before sunrise to half hour after sunset for day use

Canine compatibility: Leashed dogs permitted

Trailhead facilities: None; the B campground on the other side of the covered bridge has toilets and water.

Trail contact: Mohican State Park; (419) 994-5125; ohiodnr.gov/go-and-do/plan-a-visit/find-a-property/mohican-state-park

Special considerations: This is an extremely popular park; summer weekends are crowded, and campgrounds fill up.

Finding the trailhead: From I-71 exit 165 south of Mansfield, take SR 97 East for 15.7 miles. Just past the Mohican Memorial, turn left onto FR 51 (unmarked). Take another almost immediate left onto FR 58 (marked). Go 1.5 miles, following signs for the covered bridge. Park on the right side of the road, before crossing the covered bridge. The trailhead is on the other side of the road at a large trailhead kiosk marked "Lyons Falls Trailhead." GPS: N40 36.47' / W82 18.55'

The Hike

Mohican State Park is one of the most popular outdoor vacation destinations in Ohio. Many outings are water based, from tubing at the campground to fly fishing the Clear Fork to, of course, canoeing the Mohican River. The hike to Big and Little Lyons Falls is centered on water too, in this case the low-flowing Big Lyons and Little Lyons waterfalls. Plan to visit in late winter or early spring (or after a soaking rain) if you want to see the water really flowing.

The start of this trail is itself a destination—the covered bridge that spans the Clear Fork of the Mohican River. It looks old-fashioned but was built in 1969 to replace an old trestle bridge. From here, walk upstream on the white-blazed Lyons Falls Trail, paralleling the Clear Fork. This is one of the best trout streams in the state, so expect to see anglers from fall through spring, when the water is cool enough to

Big Lyons Falls

support a stocked trout population. In early spring look for skunk cabbage blooming near the water. Riparian birds include ducks, kingfishers, and great blue herons.

Then walk away from the river toward the falls in a mostly hardwood forest with a substantial amount of hemlock trees, which love the cool, damp areas where you find waterfalls. First arrive at Big Lyons Falls, which pours 80 feet over a shallow recess

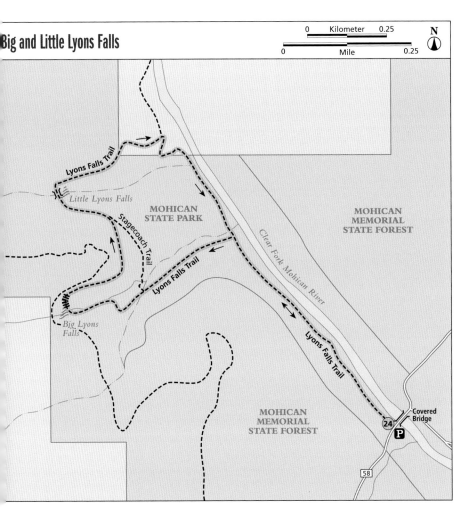

cave. Then come to Little Lyons Falls, which is shorter (25 feet) but just as attractive in its own way, pouring into a narrow sandstone chasm.

Most waterfalls are named for the stream itself, but in this case both Lyons Falls are named for pioneers who lived here and were legendary—that is, there are legends surrounding their lives and deaths. The only thing truly known is that a grave marker near Big Lyons Falls bears the name Lyons. Another legend who lived here was Johnny Appleseed (born John Chapman), who owned land in this area for apple tree nurseries. He reportedly violated Leave No Trace principles and carved his name in the soft sandstone here, which has since worn away.

Miles and Directions

0.0 Start at the trailhead kiosk by the covered bridge. Walk away from the road, paralleling the Clear Fork upstream. This is the Lyons Falls Trail, marked with white blazes.

Little Lyons Falls

0.5 Come to a four-way junction. Turn left, following a sign for the falls.

0.75 Pass a junction with the Stagecoach Trail on the right, continuing straight.

1.0 Arrive at Big Lyons Falls, then take the wooden steps out of the valley.

1.25 Come to another junction with the Stagecoach Trail on the right. Continue straight. There is a sign here for Little Lyons Falls and the dam.

1.4 Arrive at Little Lyons Falls. Cross the footbridge over the falls and continue following the white blazes.

1.7 Come to a junction and turn right, following a sign for the covered bridge.

2.0 Return to the original four-way junction. Continue straight this time.

2.5 Arrive back at the trailhead.

Hike Information

Local information: Destination Mansfield-Richland County; (419) 525-1300; destinationmansfield.com

Discover Mohican/Mohican-Loudonville Visitors Bureau; discovermohican.com

Organizations: Mohican Trails Club; mohicantrailsclub.org; twitter.com/mohicanc

Camping: Malabar Farm State Park Campground; (866) 644-6727; ohiodnr.gov/go-and-do/plan-a-visit/find-a-property/malabar-farm-state-park-campground

Mohican State Park Campground; (866) 644-6727; ohiodnr.gov/go-and-do/plan-a-visit/find-a-property/mohican-state-park-campground

25 Dundee Falls

The term "hidden gem" is an overused cliché. But in the case of Dundee Falls, it really is hidden among the vast farm fields of Amish country, and it really is quite a gem—a 15-foot-tall waterfall in a natural sandstone amphitheater. On top of that, it's not well known, so you might have the place to yourself. Add Lower Dundee Falls and other bonus waterfalls along the hike, and you've got your new favorite hidden gem in Ohio.

Height of falls: 15 feet

Type of falls: Plunge

Distance: 1.9-mile lollipop

Difficulty: Moderate due to stream crossings

Hiking time: About 1 hour

Trail names: A Trail, Falls Loop Trail

Trail surface: Dirt

Seasons and hours: Best in late winter and early spring; open Sept 1 to May 1, 6 a.m. to 8 p.m., for hiking (nonhunting, trapping, fishing activities); May 2 to Aug 31, 6 a.m. to 10 p.m., for hiking

Canine compatibility: Dogs permitted; non-hunting dogs must be leashed.

Trailhead facilities: None

Trail contact: Beach City Wildlife Area; (330) 644-2293; ohiodnr.gov/go-and-do/plan-a-visit/find-a-property/beach-city-wildlife-area

Special considerations: This area is managed for hunting. Be aware of hunting seasons, particularly deer rifle season, which generally takes place between Thanksgiving and the first week of Dec. Plan to wear hunter orange anytime you go, just to be safe. The streams may be impassable in high water, as there are no footbridges.

Finding the trailhead: From I-71 exit 165 south of Canton, take US 250 West (watch for the turn) 5 miles to Chestnut Ridge Road NW. Turn left and go 2 miles to Camp Road NW. Turn left again and go 1.6 miles to Dundee Wilmot Road. Turn left and continue 0.2 mile to the parking lot on the left, marked with a sign for the Beach City Wildlife Area. GPS: N40 36.38' / W81 37.29'

The Hike

This is a great multi-waterfall hike at an uncrowded destination. Beach City Wildlife Area is managed for hunting, trapping, and fishing. As such, in addition to the formal trails, you can hike anywhere. The waterfalls are so popular that there are well-worn paths to get you to them. Trails are named A, B, and C. Based on the occasional "A" and "B" blaze, you can tell which one you're on. The direct access to Lower Dundee Falls from Camp Road is called the Falls Loop Trail.

Begin at the gravel parking lot off Dundee Wilmot Road and take the obvious trail on the north side of the lot, marked with an "A." Within a few hundred yards, descend to an unnamed tributary to the South Fork of Sugar Creek. You'll approach Dundee Falls from upstream, hearing it before you see it. Dundee Falls is

Dundee Falls

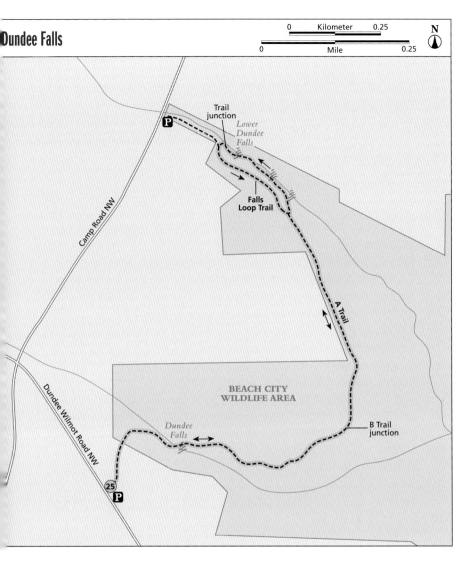

quite striking as it pours into a natural sandstone amphitheater. After checking out the falls, walk upstream again and cross the stream above the falls, looking for the "A" blaze and an occasional red blaze.

There are a lot of social trails here, but the main trail is substantial and blazed, so as long as you keep an eye out, you should be able to stay on the trail. Hike in a hardwood forest, with hemlock trees lining the cool gorges. Spring wildflowers include trillium, mayapple, and false Solomon's seal. Summer brings a plethora of jewelweed, aka spotted touch-me-not. The invasive multiflora rose has made substantial inroads here. Listen for thrushes, woodpeckers, and other songbirds.

At first you follow the creek downstream, but past Dundee Falls, at a junction with social trails and Trail B, turn left and hike in an upstream direction, along a different stream. Once you begin the Falls Loop Trail, the trail once again gets quite nice—it descends to the stream, where there are several small waterfalls along this section. The forest here has large oak trees. Cross the creek and then arrive at Lower Dundee Falls, which is almost as pretty as Dundee Falls and is a bit taller and wider. When water is high, Lower Dundee Falls produces enough flow to create a mist. Cross the creek directly below the falls. You can even walk behind the waterfall, as there is room between the bottom of the falls and the rock face. Complete the loop and then return the way you came.

Miles and Directions

0.0 Start at the trailhead located on the far side of the parking lot from the entrance, marked with a post labeled "A." In about 300 feet, the trail turns right at another "A" marker. Take this down to the creek.

0.1 Arrive at the stream and turn right, following it downstream a couple hundred feet to Dundee Falls. Turn around and cross the creek above the falls to continue on the trail.

0.4 Come to a fork with a social trail. Take the left fork, following the "A" marker.

0.5 Come to a junction with the B Trail. Take a left, staying on the A Trail.

0.9 Begin a loop at a fork where you see an "A" marker and a red blaze. Take the right fork to walk the loop in a counterclockwise direction.

1.0 At another "A" marker, cross the creek and then walk upstream to Lower Dundee Falls. Cross the creek again by the falls and ascend out of the valley.

1.1 Pass the B Trail on the right and continue straight. At an access trail, turn sharply left and walk downstream. First closely parallel the farm field; then, at a fork, take the left fork, paralleling the creek below.

1.2 Return to the junction where you started the loop. Turn right and retrace your steps to the trailhead.

1.9 Arrive back at the trailhead.

Hike Information

Local information: Tuscarawas County Convention and Visitors Bureau; (800) 527-3387; traveltusc.com

Camping: Amish Country Campsites; (330) 359-5226; amishcountrycampsites.com

Honorable Mentions

Northeast Ohio

A Mudcatcher Falls

Mudcatcher Falls isn't one of the signature waterfalls of Cuyahoga Valley National Park; in fact, this is not a natural waterfall at all. This water feature dates back to the construction of the Ohio & Erie Canal, which operated from 1827 to 1913. Gaulley Run is a waterway that fed into the canal, but in order to prevent soil and other debris from entering the canal, a "mudcatcher" was built as a filter to keep out the debris flowing down Gaulley Run. After the canal ceased operating, the soil and debris filled up the area behind the mudcatcher. Now, water flows over the mudcatcher in the form of a small waterfall. From the trailhead, walk over the Cuyahoga River on the Station Road Bridge and arrive at the Ohio & Erie Canal Towpath Trail. Turn left (north) and walk 0.5 mile to Mudcatcher Falls. Then hike any out-and-back length of your choosing: The Ohio & Erie Canal Towpath is more than 90 miles in length; 20 of those miles are within Cuyahoga Valley National Park. In summer you can check out the Hike Aboard feature of the Cuyahoga Valley Scenic Railroad for a one-way shuttle (fee). Find schedule and stops at cvsr.org/hike-aboard. This is a great birding trail, with plenty of sightings of kingfishers, great blue herons—and nesting bald eagles.

Trail contact: Cuyahoga Valley National Park; (440) 717-3890; nps.gov/cuva

Finding the trailhead: From I-77 exit 149A near Brecksville, turn east onto SR 82 and drive 3.3 miles to Riverview Road; turn right. Go 0.2 mile to Chippewa Creek Drive; continue another 0.2 mile to the Station Road Bridge parking lot on the right. Pick up the trailhead at a kiosk north of Chippewa Creek Road. GPS: N41 19.7' / W81 35.15'

B Euclid Creek Waterfalls

The 43-mile Euclid Creek is one of northeast Ohio's classic Lake Erie tributaries, with familiar tall shale cliffs. Cleveland Metroparks' Euclid Creek Reservation buffers the creek with a narrow greenspace for its last few miles before it pours into Ohio's Great Lake. While no major waterfalls exist along Euclid Creek, it drops to create a steady supply of shelf falls, cascades, and pools. During high-water events, you'll even see cascades coming down the shale cliffs that hem the creek. Also note that during high-water events, flash floods are a very real and serious danger; stay out of the creek itself. Start at the Welsh Woods Picnic Area and cross the pedestrian bridge over Euclid Creek—this is a perfect spot to look upstream for small waterfalls, pools, and swirling water. From there, walk the 1.0-mile Eastern Ledge Trail, which leads to a vista more than 100 feet above the creek. Want more mileage? Hop on the adjacent paved All Purpose Trail, which is 2.5 miles in length. Interpretive signs help you "see" in more detail the layers of Chagrin Shale, Cleveland Shale, and Euclid Bluestone, which was used for construction purposes when this area was being developed. Spring brings wildflowers, fall brings a colorful forest, but summer brings temperatures that make a swim in Lake Erie the cherry on top of your hike. Don't forget your bathing suit, as Euclid Creek Reservation includes lake access.

Trail contact: Cleveland Metroparks Euclid Creek Reservation; (216) 382-5660; clevelandmetro parks.com/parks/visit/parks/euclid-creek-reservation

Finding the trailhead: From I-90 exit 182A, turn south onto East 185th Street. Continue straight for 1.2 miles to Euclid Creek Parkway on the right. Turn into the park and continue 1.2 miles on the parkway to the Welsh Woods Picnic Area on the left. The Eastern Ledge Trail begins near the parking by the footbridge over Euclid Creek. GPS: N41 32.51' / W81 31.42'

○ Girdled Road Reservation Waterfall

If you enjoyed the hikes and shelf waterfalls at Hell Hollow Wilderness Area and Hogback Ridge Park, there is another Lake Metropark property for you: Girdled Road Reservation. The 4.1-mile Oak Leaf Loop Trail takes you along the rapidly flowing Big Creek and to a creek-spanning shelf waterfall, just a short walk upstream from the pedestrian suspension bridge, where you can get a great view of the creek. This waterfall is unnamed, but it could be called Big Creek Falls. The creek—and your hike along this section of trail—is framed by hemlock, cottonwood, and sycamore trees. Even better: You can wade in the creek, totally legal. Designated an Important Bird Area by Audubon Ohio, expect to see common ducks and geese plus birds like green herons and cedar waxwings. With a permit, you can camp at a designated campsite near Big Creek and fall asleep to the soothing sound of flowing water.

Trail contact: Lake Metroparks Girdled Road Reservation; (440) 639-7275; lakemetroparks .com/parks-trails/girdled-road-reservation

Finding the trailhead: From I-90 east of Cleveland, take exit 200 for SR 44. Go south on SR 44 for 1.5 miles to a traffic light at Girdled Road. Turn left and follow Girdled Road 2.5 miles to SR 608. Turn right (south) and go 1.8 miles to Radcliffe Road. (*Note:* You will pass the Skok Meadow entrance to the park.) Turn left (east) onto Radcliffe Road and drive 0.2 mile to the parking area on the left, marked with a large "Girdled Road Reservation" sign. Begin your hike at the trailhead kiosk for the South Meadow Trail, which takes you to the Oak Leaf Loop Trail. GPS: N41 38.31' / W81 10.31'

Central Ohio

Central Ohio is in Ohio's agricultural and urban flatlands. Because of this, waterfalls are few and far between. But they do exist! Two central Ohio waterfalls featured here are within the Columbus metropolitan area. There's Indian Run Falls (hike 27) in Columbus's northwest suburb, Dublin, and a new-to-the-public waterfall named Millikin Falls (hike 28) in Columbus's newest Metro Park–Quarry Trails. Quarry Trails is within the I-270 outerbelt, and other features include the nation's first urban *via ferrata* (protected climbing route), mountain bike trails, and a small lake for paddling. The third waterfall featured in central Ohio, Honey Run Waterfall (hike 26), is just a little more than an hour's drive from downtown Columbus. Fortunately, Columbus is centrally located, making most of the waterfalls in this book within a 2-hour drive, and many within a 1-hour drive, of the Columbus metro area.

Another well-known waterfall in central Ohio is Hayden Run Falls. It has a short boardwalk and a separate viewing platform, but no proper hiking trail. This substantial plunge is located in Dublin, the same Columbus suburb where Indian Run Falls is located. The waterfall is located in Hayden Run Falls Park; a Google maps search will get you there.

26 Honey Run Waterfall

Start in a restored wildflower prairie replete with blackberries and vistas, end at the state-designated scenic Kokosing River, and in between hike to Honey Run Waterfall. This 25-foot-tall cascade is quite substantial following rain—you'll hardly believe you're in central Ohio. This hike and waterfall would be an attraction anywhere.

Height of falls: 25 feet
Type of falls: Cascade
Distance: 2.4 miles out and back
Difficulty: Easy
Hiking time: About 1 hour
Trail names: Prairie Trail, Pine Knob Trail, Waterfall Trail
Trail surface: Mowed grass, dirt, short paved wheelchair-accessible section

Seasons and hours: Best in late June and July after a rain; open daily, 6 a.m. to 11 p.m.
Canine compatibility: Leashed dogs permitted
Trailhead facilities: Picnic area
Trail contact: Honey Run Highlands Park, Knox County Park District; (740) 392-PARK (740-392-7275); knoxcountyparks.org/parks/honey-run-waterfall/

Finding the trailhead: From the junction of US 62 and US 36 about 11 miles east of Mount Vernon, go south on US 62 for 1.3 miles to a sign for Honey Run Highlands Park. Turn left onto a gravel road and a parking lot. Continue 0.3 mile on the gravel road to a second parking lot. From here, pick up the Prairie Trail across the gravel road from the parking. It is marked with a trailhead sign. GPS: N40 22.37' / W82 16.53'

The Hike

Hats off to Knox County Park District—not only did they acquire the land around Honey Run Waterfall in 2007 and open it to the public, they've continued to improve the site since then. First they added acreage to the west of the falls and developed a tallgrass prairie; then they purchased land to extend the hiking trails east to the Kokosing River, a state-designated scenic river and water trail. Combine these features for a hike that's a study in contrasts, and in a good way.

Start on the Prairie Trail. Late June and July are great times to see prairie wildflowers like purple coneflower, black-eyed Susan, bergamot, and coreopsis. Goldenrod takes over in late summer. This is also the time to pick black raspberries and blackberries—the trail is loaded with them. Also look and listen for prairie birds. You'll see bluebird boxes and the bluebirds themselves. These boxes have also been home to tree swallows and house wrens. Look for warblers, including prairie warblers. As you come to the junction of the Prairie and Warbler Trails, take in a 360-degree view of the surrounding prairie and wooded ridges beyond. There's even a bench here for you.

The Prairie Trail ends at the intersection with the Pine Knob Trail. Turn right and take the Pine Knob Trail, as the prairie eventually turns to a young forest, all the way

Honey Run Waterfall

to the parking lot on Hazel Dell Road. Throughout the prairie section of the trail, keep an eye on your trail/mowed path. There are numerous intersecting trails and mowed firebreaks. Download the trail map in advance, keep on top of where you are at each junction, and you shouldn't get lost.

From the parking lot, cross Hazel Dell Road and come to the ADA-only parking lot. From here there is a wheelchair-accessible trail to an overlook of the falls. You can

Honey Run Waterfall

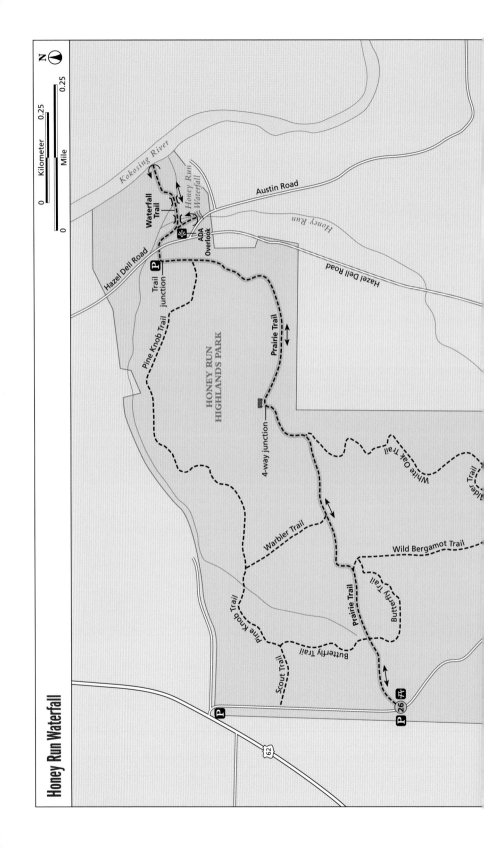

Map labels:

Kilometer 0 0.25

Mile 0 0.25

N

Kokosing River

Waterfall Trail

Honey Run Waterfall

Hazel Dell Road

Austin Road

Honey Run

ADA Overlook

Trail junction

Pine Knob Trail

HONEY RUN HIGHLANDS PARK

Prairie Trail

Hazel Dell Road

4-way junction

White Oak Trail

Warbler Trail

Alder Trail

Wild Bergamot Trail

Prairie Trail

Butterfly Trail

Pine Knob Trail

Scout Trail

Butterfly Trail

62

26

walk all the way to the falls on trails on either side of Honey Run. After checking out the falls, continue east/downstream (Honey Run takes a sharp bend) and walk to the Kokosing River. The name Kokosing is derived from the native Lenape/Delaware name for the river, *Gokhos*, which translates to "river of little owls." This section of trail is very different from the prairie; look and listen for woodland birds here, including the namesake screech owls, barred owls, and great horned owls. Hemlock trees surround the falls, as do spring wildflowers like hepatica, jack-in-the-pulpit, trout lily, and wild ginger.

You can explore along the banks of the Kokosing River, but do not attempt to swim. There are strong undercurrents, and people have drowned here. If you want to wade in the river, try the nearby Millwood River Access at the intersection of Hazel Dell Road and Bridge Street.

Miles and Directions

0.0 Start at the Prairie Trail trailhead on the east side of the gravel access road. It's marked with a sign. Follow the mowed path east.

0.2 Come to a mowed four-way junction. Continue straight.

0.25 Pass a mowed path on the right that is labeled a firebreak. Arrive at a junction; turn left to stay on the Prairie Trail. (Straight is the Bergamot Trail; both trails are signed.) After the left on the Prairie Trail, pass another firebreak in about 100 feet and trend right.

0.3 Come to a junction with the signed Warbler Trail on the left. Continue straight on the Prairie Trail.

0.4 Pass another firebreak on the right and come to a signed junction with the White Oak Trail. Turn left. You then come to what looks like a four-way junction by a bench. The trail trends right here, just past the bench, and enters a young forest.

1.0 Come to a T intersection with the signed Pine Knob Trail. Turn right onto the Pine Knob Trail.

1.1 Arrive at the parking lot and the junction with the Waterfall Trail. Turn right and walk across Hazel Dell Road. From the ADA parking lot on the other side of the road, take the trail to the falls. Below (downstream of) the waterfall, cross over a footbridge and take the Waterfall Trail east to the Kokosing River.

1.2 Come to the Kokosing River. Retrace your steps to the trailhead.

2.4 Arrive back at the trailhead.

Hike Information

Local information: Knox County Convention & Visitors Bureau; (740) 392-6102; visitknoxohio.org

Organizations: Park District Volunteers; (740) 392-PARK (740-392-7275); knoxcountyparks.org/park-district-volunteers

Camping: The Caves Campground; (740) 427-2283; carlmerritt.com/productions/cc.htm

27 Indian Run Falls

Prepare for real estate envy as you hike to Indian Run Falls, a beautiful set of two distinct waterfalls—one cascading, one plunging—in this decidedly urban-wild interface. Coming in at less than a mile in length, enjoy an easy hike to the waterfalls and then walk a few blocks to historic downtown Dublin, where you have plenty of post-hike food and drink options.

Height of falls: 22 feet; 12 feet
Type of falls: Cascade; plunge
Distance: 0.8 mile out and back
Difficulty: Easy
Hiking time: About 20 minutes
Trail name: Trail is unnamed.
Trail surface: Gravel, dirt
Seasons and hours: Best in spring and early summer; open daily, dawn to dusk

Canine compatibility: Leashed dogs permitted
Trailhead facilities: None
Trail contact: City of Dublin Park Operations; (614) 410-4700; dublinohiousa.gov/recreation-services/parks/map-your-destination/ or visitdublinohio.com/listing/indian-run-falls/382/

Finding the trailhead: From I-270 on the northwest side of Columbus, take exit 17A (US 33) and head east 0.9 mile to North High Street. Turn left (north) and go 0.1 mile to Rock Cress Parkway. Take a left and find parking on the street or in the parking garage. Near the junction of Rock Cress Parkway and Franklin Street, walk north on a wide gravel path. GPS: N40 06.07' / W83 11.57'

The Hike

Hiking to Indian Run Falls, you are constantly in reach of nature on one side and suburban development on the other. Start at Dublin Veterans Park on the corner of North High Street and Rock Cress Parkway. You'll see a large sign for Indian Run Falls with a shamrock where Dublin Veterans Park meets Indian Run Falls Park. At the trailhead kiosk by this sign, begin walking the wide gravel trail toward Indian Run. Soon you will hear the riffling waters of Indian Run. You will also hear the highway. That's the nature of a hike like this.

Walk upstream on the wide and unblazed trail and come to the occasional overlook. Although the understory in this forest is choked with honeysuckle, there are some substantial sycamore, maple, and oak trees. Listen and look for birds like woodpeckers and hawks, along with common backyard birds like cardinals, blue jays, and chickadees.

As the trail turns and crosses over Indian Run on a footbridge, you'll see some homes that will have you looking on Zillow to find out when one goes for sale. You cross where the water starts picking up speed before plunging some 22 feet over a cascading waterfall. After crossing, walk downstream to two overlook platforms. The

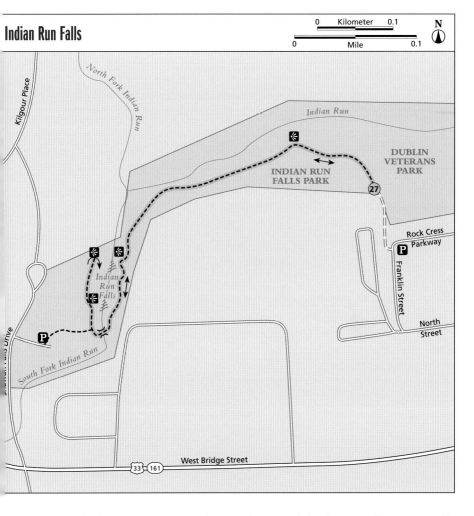

second overlook gives you an unobstructed view of the lower Indian Run Falls, which plunges into a pool. These falls are about 12 feet tall and up to 20 feet wide in high flow.

Despite what you may see other visitors doing, swimming is not allowed. People have died here. The bridge spanning the creek above the falls is closed due to injuries and deaths resulting from people jumping off it.

Just blocks from downtown Dublin, you are within walking distance of plenty of post-hike options for a drink, a meal, or Columbus's own Jeni's Splendid Ice Creams.

Miles and Directions

0.0 Start on the wide gravel path by the junction of Rock Cress Parkway and Franklin Street. Walk north, toward a large sign that reads "Indian Run Falls" and a trailhead kiosk.

0.1 The first overlook platform is to your right, where you can view Indian Run. Continue straight.

Indian Run Falls

0.3 Come to a second overlook platform on the right. You can hear and somewhat see the falls from here. Continue paralleling the stream, but stay on the main trail. The trail then turns right and you cross Indian Run on a footbridge. The trail continues downstream on the other side.

0.4 Arrive at an overlook and then a second overlook, both on the right. The second overlook has a clear view of the lower falls. Retrace your steps to the trailhead.

0.8 Arrive back at the trailhead.

Hike Information

Local information: Visit Dublin, Ohio; (614) 792-7666; visitdublinohio.com
Hiking groups: HikeOhio!; meetup.com/hiking-555
Central Ohio Hiking Club; centralohiohiking.org

28 Millikin Falls

The landscape around Millikin Falls has changed dramatically over the years, from a native forest to a limestone quarry to a metro park. But the 25-foot-high waterfall has remained a constant. Since Quarry Trails Metro Park opened in 2021, Millikin Falls is now easily accessible for the 2 million people who live in the Columbus metro area. It's also worth a road trip if you're a waterfall hunter, especially in high water, when the flow can make the falls grow to 30 feet wide.

Height of falls: 25 feet
Type of falls: Plunge
Distance: 1.5-mile loop
Difficulty: Easy
Hiking time: About 45 minutes
Trail names: Upper Millikin Falls Trail, Lower Millikin Falls Trail, Flat Rock Trail, Connector Trail
Trail surface: Asphalt, gravel, a section of floating boardwalk

Seasons and hours: Best in spring or after rain; open daily, 6:30 a.m. to dark
Canine compatibility: Leashed dogs permitted
Trailhead facilities: Porta potty
Trail contact: Columbus Metro Parks Quarry Trails Metro Park; (614) 565-1539; metroparks.net/parks-and-trails/quarry-trails

Finding the trailhead: From the junction of I-70 and I-270 on the west side of Columbus, take I-270 North 1.4 miles to exit 10 for Roberts Road. Take a right onto Roberts Road and go 0.7 mile to Dublin Road. Turn right and go 0.8 mile to Old Dublin Road, where you take a left to enter the park. Pull into the first parking lot on the right. GPS: N39 59.58' / W83 05.24'

The Hike

Beginning in the 1840s, this slice of Columbus was far from a park—it was a quarry. At one time named Marble Cliff Quarry, it was actually limestone that was quarried here. At one point it was the largest contiguous quarry in the country, and it provided stone for the Ohio Statehouse and Ohio Stadium. Keeping with the Ohio State theme, the waterfall is surrounded by buckeye trees. Visit in late April or early May to see them in bloom.

In 2018 Columbus Metro Parks purchased the property and set to developing trails and other amenities. The first phase of the park, including Millikin Falls, opened to the public in 2021. Today the park amenities—large ponds for fishing and paddling, trails, a mountain biking area, and a *via ferrata*—exist directly adjacent to housing and retail development that began construction at the same time.

Beginning at the parking lot off Old Dublin Road (these falls were known previously as Dublin Road Falls) in the Millikin Falls Area of the park, you can practically hear the falls as soon as you get out of your car. Walk the short Upper Falls Trail a couple hundred feet to an overlook where you get a great view of Millikin Falls from

Millikin Falls

above. The falls are fed by Roberts Millikin Ditch, which was created to divert the flow of the original waterway away from the quarry. Today the waterway below the falls continues to the Scioto River on the other side of the park, similar to its original course.

Descend stairs to another view of the falls below and then continue to walk downstream. This section of water below the falls is open to wading, so you can get a great view of the falls from the water. Swimming is not allowed—nor advised, as the only time water would be high enough to swim would be in flood stage anyway.

Continue walking in a downstream direction on the Millikin Falls Lower Trail, an asphalt all-purpose path. Although there are some cottonwood and locust trees here, the trail is mostly in the sun, so pack the sunscreen or consider going in the morning or evening. Circle around the water and look for water-loving birds like great blue herons, cormorants, and great egrets.

After crossing the bridge over the lake, the trail becomes the Flat Rock Trail. Walk past more fun stuff, from kayak launches to playgrounds. Then hop on the floating boardwalk and hike over Turtle Cove, keeping an eye out for those namesake turtles. Hike up to the ridge and take a sharp left, paralleling Old Dublin Road until you return to the parking lot where you started.

Miles and Directions

0.0   Start at the trailhead kiosk located on the south end of the parking lot. Walk along the wide path about 200 feet to a fork. Take the right fork to the falls overlook. Then return to the fork and walk down the steps next to the sign that reads "Lower Falls Access Ahead."

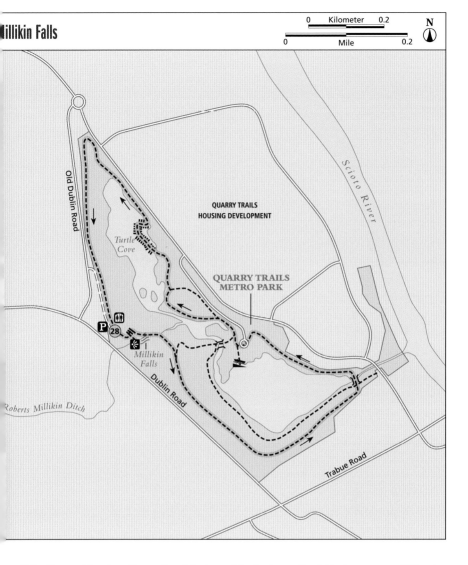

0.1 Descend the steps then arrive at the lower falls viewing on the right, down some additional steps to the water's edge. Return to the main trail and continue walking downstream.

0.2 Come to a three-way junction. Continue straight.

0.6 After passing a lake access trail on the left, turn left and walk over the first bridge you come to that crosses the lake. After crossing the bridge, take a left again.

0.8 Come to two junctions by the boat ramp. Near the boat ramp sign, take a right and go about 30 feet to the kayak launch. Take another right. (**Option:** You can turn left here and cross the lake again on another bridge to return directly to where you started.)

0.9 At a fork, take the left fork, staying by the water.

1.0 At a three-way junction by the playground, turn left. Pass an access spur to a floating dock. Take the second left and walk across the floating boardwalk.

Millikin Falls

1.1 At the end of the floating boardwalk, turn left and walk uphill on a wide gravel path.

1.25 At a three-way junction, take a right and continue uphill.

1.3 Before crossing the road, turn left and take the narrow gravel path back to the parking lot.

1.5 Arrive at the northern end of the parking lot.

Hike Information

Local information: Greater Columbus Convention & Visitors Bureau; (614) 221-6623; experiencecolumbus.com

Organizations: Friends of Metro Parks; (614) 895-6228; metroparks.net/about-us/friends-metro-parks or facebook.com/friendsofmetroparks

Hiking groups: HikeOhio!; meetup.com/hiking-555

Central Ohio Hiking Club; centralohiohiking.org

Camping: Two Columbus Metro Parks have backpacking campsites, available by reservation: Battelle Darby Creek Metro Park and Scioto Grove Metro Park. Learn more and reserve online at metroparks.net/programs-and-activities/park-activities/#backpacking.

Honorable Mention

Central Ohio

D Blackhand Gorge Waterfalls

Blackhand Gorge State Nature Preserve is home to two nice but ephemeral waterfalls. Both are unnamed. One is accessible from the Marie Hickey Trail, a loop trail north of the Licking River, which creates Blackhand Gorge. The Marie Hickey Trail is a 2.0-mile loop. Using a map with a standard orientation of north at the top, look for the waterfall at three o'clock on the loop. You'll be at the top of the falls. The other ephemeral waterfall is visible from the paved Blackhand Trail. Starting from the east end of the Blackhand Trail, walk west about 1.5 miles and look left (south) for an ephemeral waterfall, visible from the trail. Across the Licking River, you'll see a large cliff of Blackhand Sandstone. This type of sandstone got its name from a former engraved image of a black hand that was said to point toward nearby Flint Ridge, which Native Americans from different tribes accessed for its valuable flint deposits for toolmaking; reportedly it was neutral territory. The black hand engraving was destroyed when the Ohio and Erie Canal was constructed through the gorge.

Trail contact: Blackhand Gorge State Nature Preserve; (740) 763-4609; ohiodnr.gov/go-and-do/plan-a-visit/find-a-property/blackhand-gorge-state-nature-preserve

Finding the trailhead:

For the Marie Hickey Trail: From I-70 in Zanesville, take SR 146 West for 17 miles to CR 273, marked with a green sign for Toboso and Blackhand Gorge State Nature Preserve. Turn left (south) and go 1.3 miles to Rock Haven Road NE. Turn right (west) and go 1 mile to the Blackhand Gorge north parking lot on the left. GPS: N40 3.30' / W82 14.17'

For the Blackhand Trail: From I-70 in Zanesville, take SR 146 West for 17 miles to CR 273, marked with a green sign for Toboso and Blackhand Gorge State Nature Preserve. Turn left (south) and travel 1.8 miles to the parking lot on the right. GPS: N40 3.21' / W82 13.6'

Southwest Ohio

Southwest Ohio is where the generally flat, agricultural (and urban again) flatlands of Ohio meet the hills surrounding the Ohio River in the Cincinnati area. Like much of Ohio, this landscape was influenced by the last glacier, some 12,000 years ago, whether flattened by the glacier or formed by glacial deposits or melting ice. Southwest Ohio has a surprising number and variety of waterfalls. And most of them are within easy driving distance from Dayton, Cincinnati, and Columbus.

Unlike some other parts of the state, much of the bedrock here is limestone. Water more easily erodes this relatively soft stone, creating waterfalls (particularly where a harder stone like sandstone meets limestone, creating the falls) as well as gorges, like the gorge along Massies Creek (hike 34) and Clifton Gorge (hike 33). Because of this limestone base, look for spring wildflowers that you won't find common in other parts of the state, where sandstone dominates. These include wood columbine, larkspur, and shooting star.

Waterfalls in southwest Ohio are quite variable, from high-volume Greenville Falls (hike 29) to tall Charleston Falls (hike 30) to those created by full-size and/or low-head dams, like at Sharon Woods (hike 36). Southwest Ohio also has a number of high-quality waterfalls that aren't known statewide, largely due to the fact that they exist on lands held by private preserves—for example, Quiverheart Falls, operated by the Arc of Appalachia preserve system (hike 39) or Cedar Falls in the Edge of Appalachia preserve (hike 40)—or are operated by county parks (see Cedar Cliff Falls, hike 34). Without the general knowledge or marketing budget of, say, Ohio State Parks or larger Metroparks in northeast Ohio, these waterfalls continue to fly largely under the radar.

This book is an invitation for you to learn about and visit some of these lesser-known falls, and southwest Ohio has some you've probably never heard of.

29 Greenville Falls

What the trails lack in length, Greenville Falls makes up for in volume. This isn't necessarily a destination hike, but it is a destination waterfall. If you're in the area, a trip to Greenville Falls is well worth it. Enjoy a ribbon of greenway among farm fields, and take in the 125-foot-wide cascading waterfall along with historic artifacts that show the hydroelectric history here.

Height of falls: 20 feet tall, 125 feet wide
Type of falls: Cascade, tiered
Distance: 0.6-mile lollipop
Difficulty: Easy
Hiking time: About 20 minutes
Trail names: Trails are unnamed.
Trail surface: Gravel, dirt, grass

Seasons and hours: Good year-round; open daily, 8 a.m. to sunset
Canine compatibility: Leashed dogs permitted
Trailhead facilities: Porta potty, picnic table
Trail contact: Miami County Park District Greenville Falls State Scenic River Area; (937) 335-6273; miamicountyparks.com/park/greenvillefalls

Finding the trailhead: From the junction of I-75 and US 36 in Piqua, take US 36 West for 8.7 miles (watch for turns) to North Rangeline Road. Turn left and go 0.6 mile to Covington-Gettysburg Road. Turn right and go 0.1 mile to the entrance and parking on the left. GPS: N40 06.33' / W84 22.33'

The Hike

Start hiking from the gravel parking lot; within a few hundred feet, you'll be able to hear Greenville Falls before you see the large cascade. Greenville Falls State Scenic River Area is justly named—the waterfall is surprisingly big, and the flora and fauna that surround this small green space are impressive.

Hike this in the spring and the waterfall will be framed by blooming redbud trees, and native wildflowers will manage to eke out some space among the invasive honeysuckle. Look for trout lily and trillium in the wooded section of this hike. Buckeye trees are abundant. Hike to the remnants of an old dam and you will be right at the water's edge. Look for resident birds, such as swallows and great blue herons.

On-site information panels fill you in on the waterfall's history: In the late 1800s, the Falls Electric Company used the power of water to create hydroelectricity, which served local farmers. You can see the remnants of the old dam here. The bedrock is limestone, and you may also see embedded fossils if you look closely.

Prior to industrialization and forced displacement by European settlers, this was long home to the Shawnee and Miami peoples. Prehistoric peoples who lived here were the mound builders known today as the Adena and Hopewell peoples.

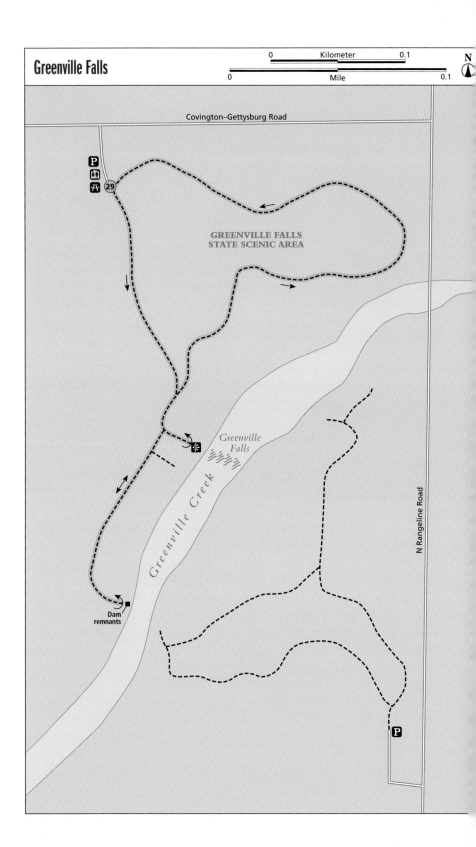

Greenville Falls

Covington–Gettysburg Road

GREENVILLE FALLS
STATE SCENIC AREA

Greenville
Falls

Greenville Creek

Dam
remnants

N Rangeline Road

0   Kilometer   0.1

0   Mile   0.1

N

29

Greenville Falls

After checking out the dam remnants, walk downstream again; pass the falls then enter the prairie section of the hike. Cedar trees dot the landscape where wild grasses and flowers dominate. Look for toadflax and golden ragwort in the spring, coneflower and butterfly weed in the summer. You'll get another good view of the falls from downstream on this section of trail.

As long as you've made the trip, go to the other side of Greenville Creek and hop on another 0.5 mile of trail. You'll be able to see other old building foundations and also a natural arch, plus more views of Greenville Falls.

Miles and Directions

0.0 Start on a wide gravel trail from the parking lot. Walk straight about 500 feet to the junction with the falls overlook spur. Go to the falls overlook; after viewing the falls, turn around and return to the main trail. Turn left. Pass a fishing access trail on the left.

0.2 The trail ends at an old dam. Turn around and retrace your steps to the falls overlook spur.

0.3 Pass the falls overlook on the right and continue straight. Almost immediately, come to a fork. Take the right fork onto the mowed path that loops through the meadow.

0.6 Arrive back at the parking lot.

Hike Information

Local information: Miami County Visitors & Convention Bureau; (800) 348-8993; homegrowngreat.com

30 Charleston Falls

The main attraction at Charleston Falls Preserve is, of course, Charleston Falls. This destination is very popular locally but not well known across the state. It should be, though. The beautiful 37-foot waterfall plunges into a pool that's surrounded by limestone cliffs, towering sycamore trees, and outstanding spring wildflowers.

Height of falls: 37 feet
Type of falls: Plunge
Distance: 1.7-mile lollipop
Difficulty: Moderate due to some steep sections
Hiking time: About 45 minutes
Trail name: Trails are unnamed.
Trail surface: Dirt, grass, gravel

Seasons and hours: Best in Apr and May; open daily, 8 a.m. to sunset
Canine compatibility: Leashed dogs permitted
Trailhead facilities: Restrooms, water, picnic area
Trail contact: Miami County Park District Charleston Preserve; (937) 335-6273; miami countyparks.com/parks/charleston

Finding the trailhead: From I-75 north of Dayton, take exit 64 onto Northwoods Boulevard and turn west a few hundred feet to Engle Road, which parallels I-75. Turn right (north) and follow Engle Road 0.6 mile to Old Springfield Road. Turn right (east) and follow Springfield Road, which becomes Ross Road, 2.3 miles to the park entrance on the left, marked with a Charleston Preserve sign. GPS: N39 54.57' / W84 08.52'

The Hike

Situated among the farm fields and cities of southwest Ohio, Charleston Falls provides both literal and figurative relief from everyday life. Plan to take your time on a hike here to explore the flora, fauna, and geology of this unique destination. This trail route takes you to both the bottom and top of Charleston Falls.

The trails are unnamed and many junctions are unmarked, so keep track of your location carefully. Start from the parking lot and picnic area and walk into a second-growth hardwood forest of maple, buckeye, and the limestone-loving hackberry, identifiable in part by its "corky" bark. Spring wildflowers are abundant here and include trillium, jack-in-the-pulpit, bloodroot, and mayapple. Ramps, or wild leeks, grow here too.

In less than 0.5 mile, arrive at a junction with steps down to the bottom of 37-foot Charleston Falls. The waterfall is spring fed but can still have low flow, so be sure to go after a good rain. Walk a boardwalk below the falls and across Charleston Creek, a tributary of the nearby Great Miami River. Then walk along the base of limestone cliffs and past a small cave in the rock. Ascend to the top of the ridge and then head west and descend into Redbud Valley. It's accurately named. Mid-April to early May, this valley is full of redbuds and dogwoods. It could just as easily be called wild ginger

Charleston Falls

valley—look for the heart-shaped leaves of wild ginger on the forest floor. If you look even closer, you can see the plant's maroon flowers, which trail on the ground.

Listen and look for birds like Carolina wrens, black-throated green warblers, and different species of woodpeckers. Slowly make your way in a clockwise direction into the Thorny Badlands, a section of pine forest. As you complete the northern loop of the trail, you'll return to Charleston Falls, this time with a bird's-eye view, looking down on the falls and the sycamores that tower over them.

Miles and Directions

0.0 Start at the trailhead kiosk past the flagpole. From here you can see a three-way junction. Walk to the junction and take a left, following the sign for the falls. In about 250 feet, the trail forks. Take the right fork.

0.3 Come to a three-way junction. Take a left and walk down wooden steps to the falls. After viewing the falls, take more wooden steps to the base of the cliff and continue straight. Pass a cave on the right.

0.5 At the top of the steps out of the gorge, turn left. The trail descends into Redbud Valley.

0.7 Come to a T intersection with a trail map. Turn right.

0.8 The trail forks. Take the right fork.

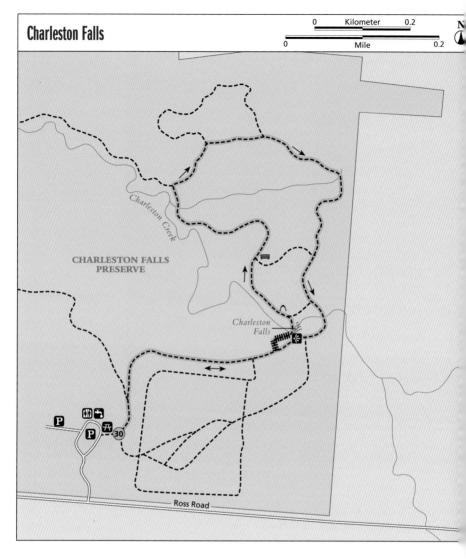

Charleston Creek

CHARLESTON FALLS PRESERVE

Charleston Falls

Ross Road

1.0 Come to a junction and continue straight.

1.1 Arrive at a junction marked with a sign for Thorny Badlands and Falls. Go left.

1.2 Arrive at a junction with a sign for Falls Overlook. Continue straight.

1.3 Come to the falls overlook to your right. Then continue straight and retrace your steps to the trailhead.

1.7 Arrive back at the trailhead.

Hike Information

Local information: Miami County Visitors & Convention Bureau; (800) 348-8993; homegrowngreat.com

Hiking groups: Dayton Hikers; daytonhikers.com

31 Oaks, Patty, and Martindale Falls

Don't think of it as a waterfall hike. Instead, think of the Green Trail at Englewood MetroPark as a nice, varied hike with three modest waterfalls along the way. Enjoy old-growth trees, bring your binoculars for birding, and set out on a hike with waterfalls in this popular Dayton/Montgomery County Five Rivers MetroPark.

Height of falls: 20, 12, and 7 feet
Type of falls: Cascade to plunge
Distance: 3.7-mile loop
Difficulty: Easy
Hiking time: About 2 hours
Trail name: Green Trail
Trail surface: Dirt
Seasons and hours: Best in winter and spring; open daily except for Christmas and New Year's

Day; Apr 1 through Oct 31, 8 a.m. to 10 p.m.; Nov 1 through Mar 31, 8 a.m. to 8 p.m.
Canine compatibility: Leashed dogs permitted
Trailhead facilities: Restrooms, water, picnic area
Trail contact: Five Rivers MetroParks Englewood MetroPark; (937) 275-PARK (7275); metroparks.org/places-to-go/englewood/

Finding the trailhead: From I-70 north of Dayton, take exit 29 and go north on SR 48 for 0.7 mile to National Road. Take a right onto National Road and head east 0.9 mile, crossing over the dam. On the other side of the dam, turn left into Englewood MetroPark. Go 0.4 mile to a stop sign. Take a right, following the sign for Patty Shelter. Drive 0.6 mile to the Patty Shelter area and parking on the right. The trailhead is located near the crosswalk. GPS: N39 52.59' / W84 17.09'

The Hike

The Patty Shelter serves as a trailhead to the whole rainbow of trails in Englewood: Black, Blue, Purple, Yellow, Red, White, and the Green Trail, which strategically takes you past three waterfalls. Each waterfall is named for a family that lived in the area during European settlement: Oakes, Patty, and Martindale. (Oakes was the family name, though the waterfall is spelled "Oaks.")

Flow can be low, so spring is the best time to visit. Hike first to Oaks Falls through a forest of Osage orange trees—note the orange-colored roots along the trail and the "monkeyballs," the tree's textured, green baseball-sized fruits. Also find some truly giant oak trees along this section of trail. Oaks Falls, like the others, pours over soft limestone rock. Throughout the hike, look and listen for birds, from resident and migrating warblers to the *who cooks for you, who cooks for you all* call of the barred owl.

Approach and cross the paved road, which was the Old National Road, the first major federal highway, built between 1811 and 1837. Soon after crossing the road, arrive at spring-fed Patty Falls. A trail spur takes you down to the falls before you continue around the top of the falls and beyond to another view from above, at a

Patty Falls

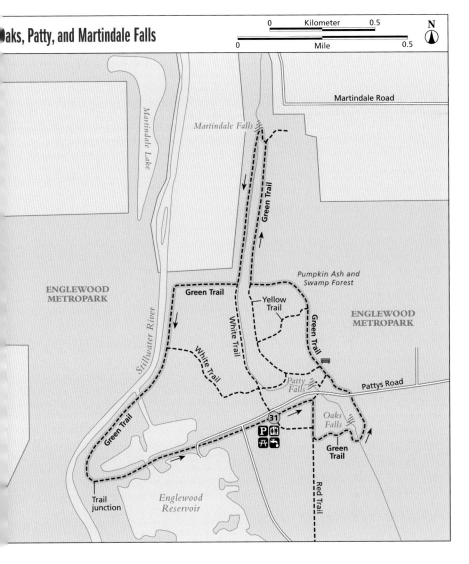

distance where Virginia bluebells frame the foreground of the falls view. Other spring wildflowers include spring beauty and bloodroot.

Before you arrive at Martindale Falls, the shortest waterfall of the three, skirt by the Pumpkin Ash and Swamp Forest—a remnant swamp forest that is a State Natural Landmark due to the relatively rare pumpkin ash trees found here. (These ash trees are seriously threatened by the emerald ash borer.) This portion of trail takes you along the edge of the limestone escarpment along the east side of the Stillwater Valley with canopy views. After checking out Martindale Falls and descending into the valley, arrive at the edge of the Stillwater River; follow it downstream, providing some of the best views of the hike. You'll see fishing access trails, but stay on the main trail until you come to another giant among trees, this time a white-barked sycamore.

Here the trail turns away from the river and finishes back at the Patty Shelter. Timing this hike can be tricky; the waterfalls generally have low flow, so going after a rain is best for waterfall viewing. However, the trail can get quite muddy, so plan ahead with appropriate footwear.

Miles and Directions

0.0 Start near the crosswalk, at the post with trail markers, including a green circle for the Green Trail. Walk east, paralleling the road. The trail crosses the grassy area and enters the woods.

0.1 Come to a junction and take a right. Keep an eye out for Green Trail blazes.

0.2 Arrive at a junction where the paved Blue Trail joins. Continue straight.

0.4 Come to a staggered four-way junction. Take a left. This is junction 17 on the map.

0.5 Arrive at the top of Oaks Falls. There is a steep spur to the bottom of the falls and back. Continue straight.

0.6 Cross the road.

0.7 Arrive at the top of Patty Falls. Take the spur trail to the left down to the falls and back. Then continue by crossing over the stream. Arrive at a junction by a bench overlooking the falls. Take a right.

1.0 Come to the junction with the Yellow Trail. Go straight, on the boardwalk.

1.2 Reach a T intersection. Turn right.

1.7 Come to a fork and take the left fork. Go downhill to Martindale Falls. At the bottom of the stairs, turn left.

2.2 Come to a junction and join the White Trail. Turn right. The trail will soon begin paralleling the Stillwater River.

2.5 At a junction where the White Trail turns left, go straight, continuing to parallel the river on the Green Trail.

3.0 Come to a fork with a social trail by a huge sycamore tree. Take the left fork and walk away from the river.

3.4 The trail arrives at the pavement and a parking area. Continue straight, walking on the pavement.

3.5 Come to a junction with Patty Road. Continue straight.

3.7 Arrive back at the trailhead.

Hike Information

Local information: Dayton Convention & Visitors Bureau; (937) 226-8211; dayton cvb.com

Hiking groups: Dayton Hikers; daytonhikers.com

Camping: Englewood is home to four campsites, available by reservation. Visit metro parks.org/rentals-permits/reserve-a-campsite, or call (937) 275-7275.

32 The Cascades

Legend has it that if you drink from the Yellow Spring, you will always return. The beauty of Glen Helen Preserve will make you want to come back anyway. Enjoy a hike that takes you past the Yellow Spring, which is like a mini waterfall unto itself, and then to The Cascades, the largest waterfall in a preserve that has many ephemeral falls in spring in addition to wildflowers and rock outcroppings.

Height of falls: 10 feet
Type of falls: Plunge
Distance: 4.0-mile loop
Difficulty: Moderate due to length and stream crossings
Hiking time: About 2 hours
Trail names: Inman Trail, Lower Birch Creek Trail, Talus Trail, Pawpaw Trail
Trail surface: Dirt

Seasons and hours: Best in spring; open daily, dawn to dusk
Canine compatibility: Leashed dogs permitted; you must clean up after your pet.
Trailhead facilities: Porta potties; restrooms and water when the museum is open
Trail contact: Glen Helen Nature Preserve; (937) 769-1902; glenhelen.org
Special considerations: There is a parking fee.

Finding the trailhead: From SR 68 in Yellow Springs, turn east onto Corry Street (on the north side of town) and travel 0.4 mile to the parking area on the left, marked with a sign. Park and then walk past the parking lot kiosk about 50 feet to the museum. GPS: N39 48.05' / W83 53.08'

The Hike

Go back to school at Glen Helen—nature school, that is. The Glen was originally associated with Antioch College; Antioch alum Hugh Taylor Birch donated the land to the college in memory of his daughter Helen. Today it is a private preserve owned by the Glen Helen Association. True to its roots in education, Glen Helen operates as a preserve but also as an environmental education center, complete with school visits, nature programming, and a raptor center. Be sure to check the schedule before visiting.

Take a hike that is centered on water, whether it's cascading creeks, springs, or waterfalls. Begin at the museum. If it's open, stop in and learn more about the surroundings you are about to observe on your hike. Hike the popular Inman Trail, which will take you past Pompey's Pillar (a dolomite limestone column), The Grotto, and then the famous Yellow Spring. Flowing at a rate of 60 gallons per minute, the spring is like a small waterfall, pouring into a pool. It is really orange in color, due to the high concentration of iron.

Past the Yellow Spring, come to the other main attraction: The Cascades. This waterfall is a classic plunge along Birch Creek, and it can be quite voluminous in the spring and after a heavy rain. Walk a spur from the main trail to a spot where you get

The Cascades

the best view of The Cascades. Across the creek from the viewing spot is another, unnamed waterfall. After crossing Birch Creek, walk downstream to the confluence with Yellow Springs Creek. Enjoy cascading water, ephemeral waterfalls, dolomite limestone rock outcroppings, and wildflowers. In spring look for limestone-loving flowers like wood columbine in addition to trillium, jack-in-the-pulpit, and other spring wildflowers. Listen for the song of the wood thrush and other birds.

Hike downstream and then back upstream along Yellow Springs Creek in an oak-hickory forest with plenty of other tree species, including the tulip tree, whose elegant leaf structure also serves as the Glen's logo. Invasive plants also have a foothold here. If you live nearby, consider volunteering for trail maintenance or invasive plant removal. Unlike public parks, the Glen is not supported by taxpayer dollars. Donations of time and/or money are needed to ensure a long future for this special place.

The Cascades

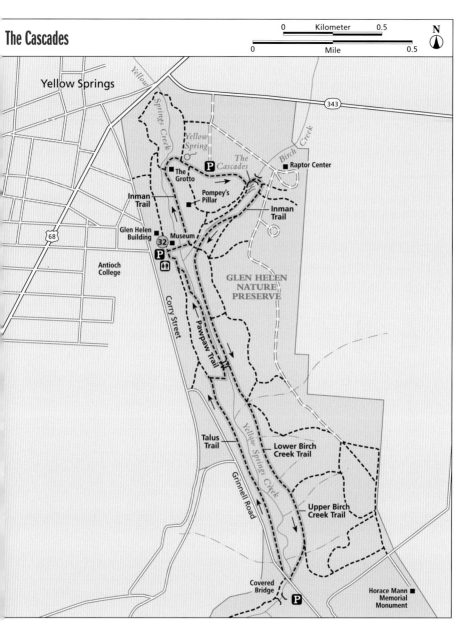

0 Kilometer 0.5

0 Mile 0.5

N

Yellow Springs

Yellow Springs Creek

343

Yellow Spring

The Cascades

Birch Creek

The Grotto

P

Raptor Center

Inman Trail

Pompey's Pillar

Inman Trail

68

Glen Helen Building

Museum

32

P

Antioch College

GLEN HELEN NATURE PRESERVE

Corry Street

Pawpaw Trail

Talus Trail

Lower Birch Creek Trail

Yellow Springs Creek

Grinnell Road

Upper Birch Creek Trail

Covered Bridge

P

Horace Mann Memorial Monument

Miles and Directions

0.0   Start at the museum and take the Inman Trail. Walk down a few stairs to a junction. Continue straight down the stone steps.

0.1   Cross a footbridge over Yellow Springs Creek. In about 150 feet come to a T intersection; turn left.

0.2   A side trail to the right takes you to Pompey's Pillar. Continue straight.

0.3 Pass a footbridge on the left atop an old cement dam. A waterfall is on the right. Continue straight.

0.5 An access trail comes in from the left. Continue straight to the Yellow Spring. About 100 feet past the spring, come to a junction. Continue straight, passing a side trail on the right.

0.7 Come to a fork. Look left and see the footbridge you will cross over the top of The Cascades. But first take a short side trip to the right and down the stairs to check out the best viewing spot for The Cascades. Return to this junction and cross the creek right above The Cascades. Then take the first trail on the right. Slowly descend toward the creek, crossing a tributary along the way.

1.0 Come to a fork. Turn right and finish the descent into the valley.

1.2 Come to a four-way junction. Continue straight and hike downstream on the Lower Birch Creek Trail. (**Option:** Turn right and cross the creek over stepping stones to return directly to the museum.)

1.5 A side trail comes in from the left. Continue straight.

1.7 Pass a footbridge over the creek on the right.

1.8 The trail turns away from the creek, crosses a tributary over stepping stones, and then forks. Take the right fork, staying near the creek. Over the next 0.5 mile, various formal and informal trails crisscross. Stay always near the creek.

2.5 Come to Grinnell Road. Turn right and cross over Yellow Springs Creek on the road; turn right on the trail again and reenter the woods. Now on the west side of the creek, hike upstream on the Talus Trail.

3.1 Cross a footbridge over a cascading tributary then almost immediately come to a fork. Turn right to stay near the creek.

3.4 Approach a fork. Turn right and descend to the creek. Walk over a boardwalk and then a bridge, then come to a four-way intersection. Turn left, continuing upstream on the west side of the creek on the Pawpaw Trail.

3.7 A side trail joins from the left. Look across the creek for cascading water and rock shelves.

3.9 Ascend to a T intersection. Turn right. Check out the cliffs to the left, but keep generally below the rocks to stay on the trail.

4.0 The trail follows a 5-foot gap between two dolomite blocks. From here, ascend the slope to the lawn by the museum, arriving back where you began.

Hike Information

Local information: Yellow Springs, Ohio (Greene County, Ohio Convention & Visitors Bureau); (937) 767-2686; yellowspringsohio.org

Organizations: Glen Helen Association; (937) 769-1902; glen-helen-association.square.site

Glen Helen Raptor Center; (937) 767-6656; glenhelen.org/raptor-center

Hiking groups: Dayton Hikers; daytonhikers.org

Camping: John Bryan State Park campground; (866) 644-6727; ohiodnr.gov/go-and-do/plan-a-visit/find-a-property/john-bryan-state-park-campground

33 Amphitheater Falls

Clifton Gorge is all about water—the Little Miami River carved the soft limestone to create the gorge itself, and on this beautiful hike you will consistently see the power of water and gravity at work. Start upstream and walk along the cliff top past narrow chutes of rushing water and then down into the gorge itself where it widens. Before you exit the gorge, hike past Amphitheater Falls, which pours over the rim of the cliff and into the gorge. Spring brings high water flow and spectacular wildflowers.

Height of falls: 25 feet
Type of falls: Plunge; ephemeral
Distance: 2.0-mile lollipop
Difficulty: Moderate due to steep sections
Hiking time: About 1 hour
Trail names: Narrows Trail, John L. Rich Trail, North Rim Trail
Trail surface: Dirt, stone

Seasons and hours: Best in spring; open daily, half hour before sunrise to half hour after sunset
Canine compatibility: Dogs not permitted
Trailhead facilities: None
Trail contact: Clifton Gorge State Nature Preserve; (937) 767-7947; ohiodnr.gov/go-and-do/plan-a-visit/find-a-property/clifton-gorge-state-nature-preserve

Finding the trailhead: From I-70 in Springfield, turn south onto SR 72 (exit 54) and drive 6.6 miles to SR 343. Turn right onto SR 343 and in 0.1 mile turn left onto Jackson Street. The parking lot for Clifton Gorge State Nature Preserve is on the right. The address is 169 Jackson Street, Clifton, Ohio. GPS: N39 47.66' / W83 49.73'

The Hike

The Little Miami is a state and national scenic river. But you don't need any designations to tell you as much—you'll see it with your own eyes. After the last glacier receded some 12,000 years ago, waters carved the dolomite limestone into what we today call Clifton Gorge. It's beautiful any time of the year, but come in spring to experience the power of rushing water and see choice wildflowers. Even many of the trees and shrubs are in bloom, including redbud and black haw viburnum.

Beginning in Clifton Gorge State Nature Preserve, walk downstream on the Narrows Trail and parallel the river closely. (A larger parking lot is located nearby on SR 343 if the trailhead lot is full.) At first you'll be walking a trail along the rim of the river, looking below to the water hemmed in by steep cliffs on either side, giving it the name of the Narrows. Late fall to early spring, when the leaves are off the trees, is a great time to get the best views of the water along this section. Stop at a series of overlooks, some with interpretive signs that help you recognize remnants showing the history of this area. There were at least five water-powered mills operating here in the 1800s. Just upstream, the Clifton Mill is still in operation and sometimes open for

Amphitheater Falls

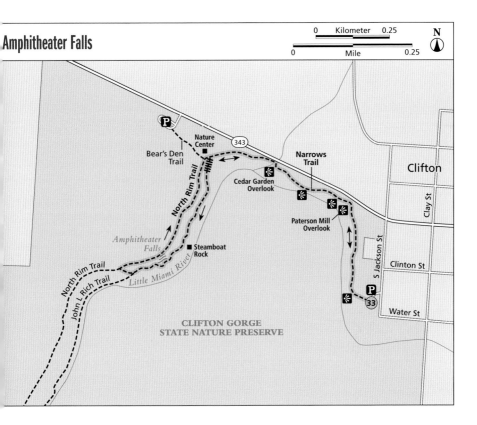

tours. It's worth a visit, particularly during the holiday season with its extensive light show (there is a fee to enter then).

Prior to pioneers and their mills, this area was home to the Shawnee people, including one of their greatest leaders, Tecumseh. Nearby were the Miami people, for whom the Miami and Little Miami Rivers are named. With European settlement, the Pittsburgh-Cincinnati Stagecoach Road was established. Today it is a trail that parallels the Little Miami just downstream of Clifton Gorge in John Bryan State Park.

Near the Bear's Den interpretive area and Clifton Gorge Nature Center, take wooden steps down into the gorge. If it's open, be sure to stop in at the nature center. Ask to see the photo of Muggins, the bear that once lived here, hence the name of the interpretive area. At the bottom of the gorge, begin walking along the John L. Rich Trail. Spring wildflowers are dense here and include snow trillium, Solomon's seal, Virginia bluebells, wild ginger, and much more. Continue downstream beneath the limestone cliffs and slump blocks (a sign tells you when you are looking at a named slump block, Steamboat Rock). Then you'll approach Amphitheater Falls, which isn't on the Little Miami but rather comes off a tributary known as Timmy's Trickle. The falls pour over the limestone cliff and the water from the falls then joins the river. After the falls, hike out of the gorge and walk upstream along the North Rim Trail back to the Narrows Trail and the trailhead.

Note: Dogs are not permitted in state nature preserves, including Clifton Gorge. If you'd like to bring your best friend, leashed dogs are allowed in the adjacent John Bryan State Park.

Miles and Directions

0.0 Start at the trailhead kiosk and walk downstream on the Narrows Trail. You will come to a series of viewing platforms that overlook Clifton Gorge and the Little Miami River.

0.6 At the nature center, a set of wooden steps takes you down to the river. Take a left here and descend the steps; you are now on the John L. Rich Trail.

0.9 Arrive at Amphitheater Falls. Continue straight.

1.0 The trail forks. Take the right fork and ascend out of the gorge on the connector to the North Rim Trail. Toward the top of the gorge is a second junction. Take a right onto the North Rim Trail.

1.4 Come to a multi-point junction with a kiosk labeled "The Bear's Den." The nature center is past this kiosk, as are the wooden stairs you took down to the gorge. Continue straight and retrace your steps on the Narrows Trail to the trailhead.

2.0 Arrive back at the trailhead.

Hike Information

Local information: Greene County, Ohio Convention & Visitors Bureau; (937) 429-9100; greenecountyohio.org

Organizations: Friends of John Bryan State Park; (937) 767-1274; facebook.com/people/Friends-of-John-Bryan-State-Park/100064445121314/

Hiking groups: Dayton Hikers; daytonhikers.org

Camping: John Bryan State Park campground; (866) 644-6727; ohiodnr.gov/go-and-do/plan-a-visit/find-a-property/john-bryan-state-park-campground

34 Cedar Cliff Falls

When you view the uniform lip of Cedar Cliff Falls, it looks like a dam created this beauty. That's because it did. The dam erected on Massies Creek in the late 1800s created the falls, which has since been joined by naturalized falls on either side. The result is an unusual and beautiful waterfall that has a powerful flow in late winter and early spring. Easy access to the falls plus a hike along the beautiful Massies Creek Gorge make for a worthwhile road trip to this county park that is under the radar statewide, but shouldn't be.

Height of falls: About 18 feet tall, 25 feet wide
Type of falls: Block
Distance: 3.1 miles out and back
Difficulty: Easy
Hiking time: About 1.5 hours
Trail names: Rim Trail, Gorge Trail, Mound Trail
Trail surface: Dirt with some sections of pavement and boardwalk

Seasons and hours: Best in Mar and Apr; open daily, sunrise to sunset
Canine compatibility: Leashed dogs permitted
Trailhead facilities: Restrooms, reservable picnic shelter
Trail contact: Greene County Parks & Trails Indian Mound Reserve; (937) 562-6440; gcparkstrails.com/parks/indian-mound-reserve/

Finding the trailhead: From Cedarville, take US 42 South 0.6 mile to the trailhead parking on the right, marked with a sign for Cedar Cliff Falls. GPS: N39 44.16' / W83 49.00'

The Hike

Geology, history, and botany are all on display at Cedar Cliff Falls. Massies Creek Gorge was created from meltwaters of the last glacier, some 12,000 years ago. Today, dolomite limestone cliffs rise above both sides of the creek and water rushes through. Look closely for pockets, slump blocks, and other features where water and stone meet.

The hike starts near Cedar Cliff Falls and has great access, including an ADA-accessible trail and overlook. You'll see this is not an entirely natural waterfall when you note the very even lip, indicating a low-head dam. This dam was built in the late nineteenth century when a mill was constructed here. Note the arch shape of the dam, giving it more strength against the current—which clearly worked, as it still stands today. The mill, or rather mills (paper mill, gristmill), obviously no longer stands. On either side of the dam, naturalized waterfalls have sprung.

Since this area was developed for industry and agriculture, it is no surprise that many of the spring flowers you'll see near the waterfall are invasive or cultivars, like mustard or dame's rocket. They are still quite beautiful, though, and frame the scene well. As you hike downstream along the gorge, native wildflowers abound. Early spring wildflowers are particularly exceptional here, including snow trillium

Cedar Cliff Falls

and skunk cabbage, which both usually bloom in March. Although it's named Cedar Cliff Falls, there are very few cedars here. There is some similar-looking American arborvitae, which is state-listed as a potentially threatened species.

As you walk downstream, take a side trip on the Mound Trail to Williamson Mound. It was named for the person who donated this land to the county, but the actual mound builders were the prehistoric Adena culture (circa 500 BCE to 100 CE), of which we don't know much, not even the name they called themselves. But they left a legacy of mounds in the Ohio Valley, and this is a particularly large and well-kept one. The trail ends at an old log house, estimated to have been built around 1814. It was reconstructed and relocated here. On the hike back, consider taking the Gorge Trail to its end before joining the Rim Trail, which keeps you closer to the water.

Miles and Directions

0.0 Start on the asphalt trail from the parking lot, marked with a large trail map. Follow it across the bridge over Massies Creek and come to a junction where the Falls Trail and Rim Trail diverge. Take a right and walk to the falls overlook.

0.1 Arrive at the overlook for Cedar Cliff Falls. Turn around and walk downstream to meet the Rim Trail again. Continue straight, paralleling the creek downstream.

0.3 Pass a spur trail that takes you down to Massies Creek. Continue straight. (**Option:** The out-and-back spur down to the creek is worth checking out first.)

Cedar Cliff Falls

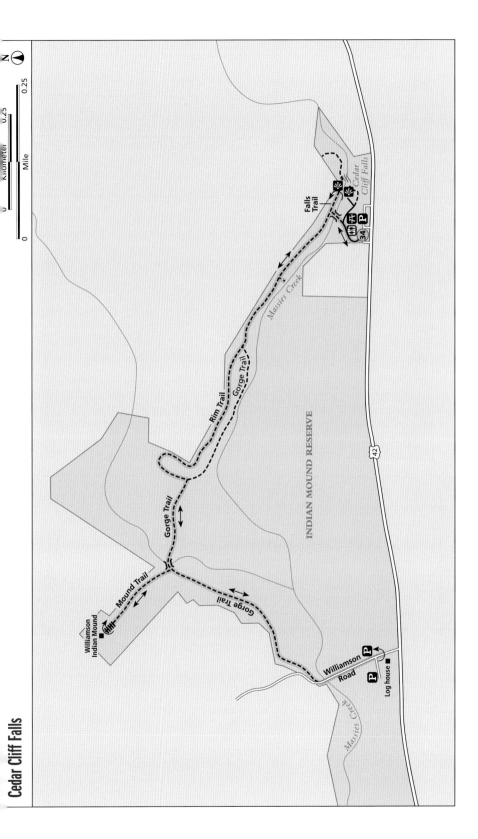

Cedar Cliff Falls

0.4 Come to a junction with the Gorge Trail. Continue straight.

0.8 Come to a T intersection and the end of the Rim Trail. Take a right onto the Gorge Trail.

1.0 Arrive at a junction with the Mound Trail. Take a right and hike the trail to the top of Williamson Mound and back.

1.3 Return to the junction with the Gorge Trail. Bear right this time.

1.6 The dirt trail ends at a road. Take a left and walk along the edge of the road then over the bridge.

1.7 Arrive at the Gorge Trail trailhead parking and the log house. Turn around here and walk directly back to the trailhead on the Gorge and Rim Trails.

3.1 Arrive back at the trailhead.

Hike Information

Local information: Greene County, Ohio Convention & Visitors Bureau; (937) 429-9100; greenecountyohio.org

Camping: John Bryan State Park campground; (866) 644-6727; ohiodnr.gov/go-and-do/plan-a-visit/find-a-property/john-bryan-state-park-campground

35 Horseshoe Falls

As promised by its name, this wide waterfall has an arching shape reminiscent of a horseshoe. April brings good flow and redbud trees framing the falls. Add a suspension bridge that takes you over the creek and more miles of adjacent trail, and you've got a nice spring waterfall hike destination in a park with practically endless other activities.

Height of falls: About 3 feet tall, up to 30 feet wide
Type of falls: Shelf
Distance: 1.8 miles out and back
Difficulty: Easy
Hiking time: About 1 hour
Trail name: Horseshoe Falls Trail
Trail surface: Dirt

Seasons and hours: Best in Apr; open daily, 6 a.m. to 11 p.m.
Canine compatibility: Leashed dogs permitted
Trailhead facilities: Restrooms, water
Trail contact: Caesar Creek State Park; (937) 728-2426; ohiodnr.gov/go-and-do/plan-a-visit/find-a-property/caesar-creek-state-park

Finding the trailhead: From I-71 exit 36 in Oregonia, turn north to Wilmington Road and take a right. Go 0.3 mile to Olive Branch Road. Turn left and go 0.4 mile to Jeffery Road. Turn right and continue 3.3 miles to Oregonia Road. Turn right and go 1.2 miles to the park entrance on the left. Turn into the park and drive 0.6 mile to the Wellman Meadows trailhead parking on the left. Pick up the trailhead at a kiosk at the far end of the parking lot, along the cul-de-sac. GPS: N39 29.08' / W84 02.56'

The Hike

Begin the hike in an open forest of cedar trees and an understory choked with honeysuckle. The flow of Horseshoe Falls is highest in late winter or spring after a rain, but trails can be muddy in wet conditions, so bring shoes that can handle the mud. As you hike, the forest gradually improves. Soon you'll see Caesar Creek Lake on your right. You'll follow the inlet to the point where it is no longer the lake but the Flat Fork, one of the tributaries that feed the lake.

The forest here is lovely in the spring. Look for wildflowers like larkspur, bloodroot, phlox, and jack-in-the-pulpit. Trees now include a largely maple forest with tall, white-barked sycamores lining the run. Redbuds and dogwoods blossom here in the spring. Arrive at the edge of Horseshoe Falls, a wide, plunging shelf waterfall that is curved, reminiscent of the shape of a horseshoe, though not nearly as curved as an actual horseshoe. In April, redbuds complete the scene where they blossom near the falls. Look and listen for water-loving birds like kingfishers. Also look closely at the limestone bedrock, which contains many fossils. Continue walking upstream for another minute and you'll come across a swinging pedestrian bridge; it's fun to walk over and gives you another view of the Flat Fork. Continue to the other side of Horseshoe Falls, which provides a substantially different view.

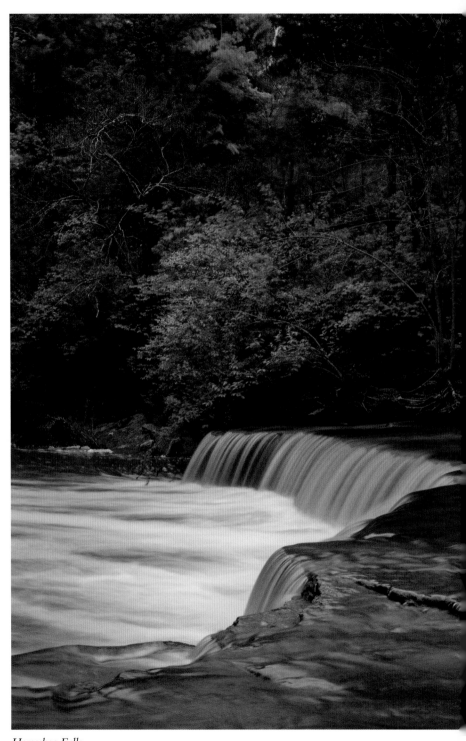

Horseshoe Falls

Horseshoe Falls

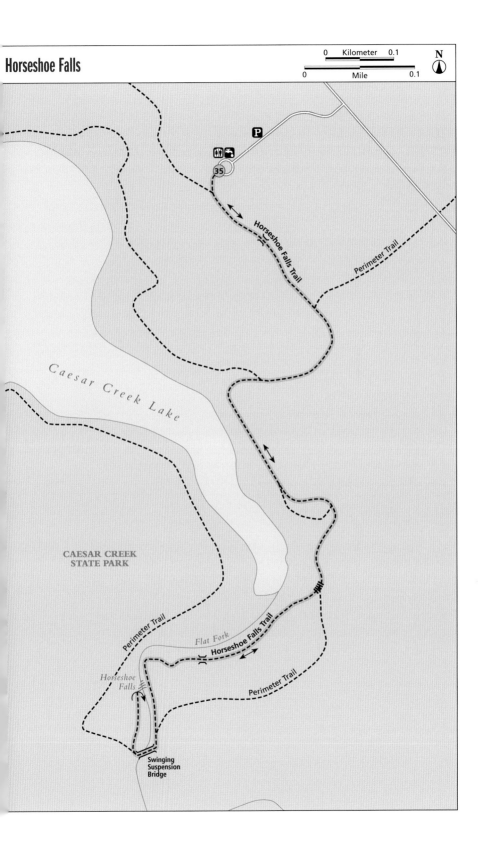

0   Kilometer   0.1

0   Mile   0.1

N

P

35

Horseshoe Falls Trail

Perimeter Trail

Caesar Creek Lake

CAESAR CREEK
STATE PARK

Perimeter Trail

Flat Fork

Horseshoe Falls Trail

Perimeter Trail

Horseshoe
Falls

Swinging
Suspension
Bridge

While you're at the park, there's plenty to do, including legal fossil hunting (with a permit). Camping, paddling, mountain biking, and a nature center make this a good family destination beyond this hike. The US Army Corps of Engineers also has a visitor center on-site, where you can learn about the dam as well as the area's rich Native American history.

While you're here, a second small waterfall can be found at Caesar Creek: Crawdad Falls. You can access Crawdad Falls from the Perimeter Trail along Jonas Run near Lukens Road.

Miles and Directions

0.0 Start at the trailhead kiosk and walk through an arbor with benches. Take the trail about 75 feet to a T intersection. Turn left, following the blue blaze.

0.1 At a junction, continue straight.

0.25 Come to another junction, continue straight. Cross a footbridge, following the blue blazes.

0.4 The trail forks but is unmarked. Take the left fork, staying on the more well-trodden path. The trail comes back together in about 200 feet. This time, continue straight, following the blue blaze.

0.6 At a junction, turn right, following the blue blaze and walking toward the stream.

0.7 Take steps down to the creek. At the creek, come to a T intersection at a boardwalk. Turn left and walk upstream.

0.75 Arrive at Horseshoe Falls.

0.8 Turn right and cross the Flat Fork over a pedestrian suspension bridge. After crossing the bridge, turn right onto a side trail and walk downstream until you can view the falls again.

0.9 Arrive at other side of Horseshoe Falls. Retrace your steps to the trailhead.

1.8 Arrive back at the trailhead.

Hike Information

Local information: Warren County Convention & Visitors Bureau; (800) 791-4FUN (4386); ohioslargestplayground.com

Organizations: Nature Center Association of Caesar Creek Lake; (513) 855-2120; caesarcreekstatepark.com

Friends of Caesar Creek; (513) 897-1050; friendsofcaesarcreeklake.org

Caesar Creek Campground Friends; facebook.com/CaesarCreekCampgroundFriends

Camping: Caesar Creek State Park campground; (866) 644-6727; ohiodnr.gov/go-and-do/plan-a-visit/find-a-property/caesar-creek-state-park-campground

36 Sharon Woods Waterfalls

The short length of Sharon Creek, which flows through Sharon Woods park, contains a spillway, two natural waterfalls, and two falls created by low head dams. Walk a flat, wide nature trail to three of these features while taking in the sights and sounds of rushing water, songbirds, wildflowers, and fossils. Before leaving the park, be sure to check out Buckeye Falls as well.

Height of falls: About 8 feet; 4 feet
Type of falls: Cascade; plunge
Distance: 1.4 miles out and back
Difficulty: Easy
Hiking time: About 30 minutes
Trail name: Gorge Trail
Trail surface: Gravel
Seasons and hours: Best in spring; open daily, dawn to dusk

Canine compatibility: Leashed dogs permitted
Trailhead facilities: None; full facilities elsewhere in the park
Trail contact: Sharon Centre; (513) 563-4513; greatparks.org/parks/sharon-woods
Special considerations: You must pay for a day pass or annual pass to enter.

Finding the trailhead: From the junction of I-275 and US 42 on the north side of Cincinnati, take US 42 South 0.7 mile to the park entrance. Turn left (east) and go 0.1 mile to Buckeye Falls Drive. Turn left and go 1 mile to the parking lot on the right. From the parking lot, backtrack by walking on the road shoulder about 150 feet to the trailhead, which enters the woods before you get to the stone bridge. GPS: N39 16.94' / W84 23.34'

The Hike

Located within Cincinnati's outerbelt, the Gorge Trail in Sharon Woods has a surprisingly backcountry feel. Except for the sound of nearby traffic, you can feel far away from it all. The trail begins at the Sharon Lake spillway—a sort of human-made waterfall that is quite attractive with its stone arch architecture and swirling water. Being lake fed means that Sharon Creek generally has decent water flow, feeding the downstream waterfalls.

Hike downstream in a forest dominated by maple trees, with sycamores near the water and flowering dogwood trees in the spring. Spring also brings nice wildflowers, including phlox, waterleaf, Solomon's seal, and wild ginger. Soon you'll arrive at a wooden overlook platform that gives you a good view of the first, and larger, cascading waterfall.

Continue downstream and cross Sharon Creek on a footbridge. Get a good look at the creek and keep an eye out for birds, including ducks swimming in the creek. Continue downstream and you'll see—and smell—anise root. Arrive at a second waterfall, also spanning the width of the creek. Although shorter, it has a more precipitous plunge than the upper waterfall.

A waterfall along Sharon Creek

There is still a little bit of trail left. Continue to the end and you'll see quite a bit of spiderwort here in the spring. Now that you are closer to the creek, inspect the limestone for ancient fossils. Please leave what you see so others can also enjoy the fossils, which include brachiopods and trilobites. End at Buckeye Falls Drive and turn around to retrace your steps to the trailhead. The name Buckeye Falls Drive is derived from a waterfall that is downstream from here. Before you leave the park, check out two more waterfalls created by low-head dams, visible by parking at lots along Buckeye Falls Drive and walking over to the creek. Buckeye Falls is the one nearest to the Heritage Village buildings.

Miles and Directions

0.0 Start at the eastern terminus about 150 feet from the parking lot by the Sharon Lake spillway. Walk away from the road into the woods.

0.1 Come to an overlook platform for the first waterfall along Sharon Creek. Continue walking downstream.

0.4 Cross Sharon Creek on a footbridge.

0.6 Arrive at the second waterfall along Sharon Creek. Continue walking downstream.

0.7 The trail ends at Buckeye Falls Drive. Retrace your steps to the trailhead.

1.4 Arrive back at the trailhead.

Sharon Woods Waterfalls

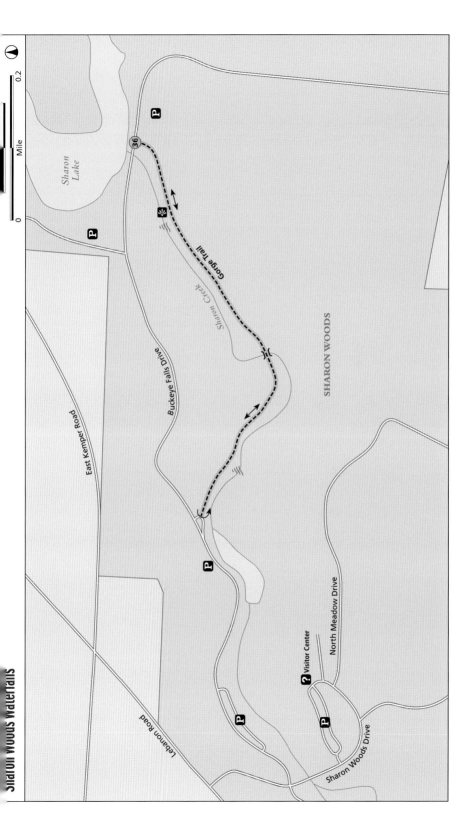

SHARON WOODS

Sharon Lake

East Kemper Road

Lebanon Road

Buckeye Falls Drive

Sharon Creek

Gorge Trail

Visitor Center

North Meadow Drive

Sharon Woods Drive

36

Mile

0   0.2

A waterfall along Sharon Creek

Hike Information

Local information: Visit Cincy; (513) 621-2142; visitcincy.com
Hiking groups: Tri-State Hiking Club; meetup.com/hike-cincinnati
Camping: Great Parks of Hamilton County has several campgrounds. The two closest to Sharon Woods are Winton Woods and Lake Isabella; greatparks.org/recreation/camping.

37 Fallsville Falls

Fallsville Falls offers an unusual opportunity in the state—you can hike off-trail, explore the falls, and wade across the creek. Plan to come in warm weather but after a rain, as these are generally low-flow falls. However, flow can be quite high in late winter to early spring.

Height of falls: 15 feet tall, 25 feet wide
Type of falls: Tiered
Distance: 0.6 mile out and back
Difficulty: Moderate due to steep fall-line trail down to the water
Hiking time: About 20 minutes
Trail name: No official trails
Trail surface: Dirt
Seasons and hours: Best in early summer after a good rain; open daily, half hour before sunrise to half hour after sunset

Canine compatibility: Dogs permitted; must be leashed May 1 through Aug 31
Trailhead facilities: None
Trail contact: Fallsville Wildlife Management Area; (937) 372-9261; ohiodnr.gov/go-and -do/plan-a-visit/find-a-property/fallsville -wildlife-area
Special considerations: It's best to avoid this area altogether during deer gun season, which generally begins the Monday after Thanksgiving and lasts a week. It is always a good idea to wear hunter-orange clothing.

Finding the trailhead: From US 50 in Hillsboro, take SR 73 West 2.3 miles to Carl Smith Drive. Turn right and drive 0.3 mile to a roundabout. Take the third exit from the roundabout to go north on Careytown Road. Continue 3.7 miles to a gravel parking lot on the left marked with a sign that reads "Waterfall." GPS: N39 17.07' / W83 37.48'

The Hike

You might be surprised to find a decent-sized waterfall in the middle of Highland County farmland, but here it is in a place that was once called Fallsville. The old town was home to a gristmill powered by the waterfall. Today it's a wildlife management area intended for hunting and trapping, with no official trails. The waterfall is so popular, however, that there is a very clear trail from the parking lot to the falls.

Begin walking along a gravel road through fields that are maintained for wildlife like deer and wild turkey. This is a dog-friendly destination, and most times of the year your best friend can go off-leash. But you're required to keep your dog on a leash May through August in order to protect ground-nesting birds like quail and turkey. As you enter the woods, the road becomes a footpath. Walk by one of the on-site ponds (you'll likely be able to spot bass and bluegill) and continue on; shortly you'll hear the sound of the waterfall.

There are a number of social trails here; the well-trod trail to the falls is clear but steep. Exercise caution, especially when the ground is wet. Head down into a beautiful gorge, where moss-covered limestone rocks create natural steps into the creek.

Fallsville Falls

Take a close look at the limestone to find fossils, but leave them as they are so others can enjoy them.

The real beauty of this wildlife management area is its management. Since there are no official trails, hiking "off-trail" is allowed. Make sure your off-trail hiking and navigation skills are good. Avoid hiking alone, and make sure someone knows your plans and when you expect to return home.

While swimming is not allowed, you can explore all along Clear Creek. Flow can get low in the summer, so plan to go after a good rain. Winter and spring are best for waterfall viewing; summer is best for exploring the creek.

Miles and Directions

- **0.0** Start at the parking lot by the road. Walk west along the gravel road. (**Note:** If there is no chain across the gravel road, you can drive to the second parking area.)
- **0.2** Pass a second small parking area on the left. Continue straight as the gravel road narrows to a dirt trail.

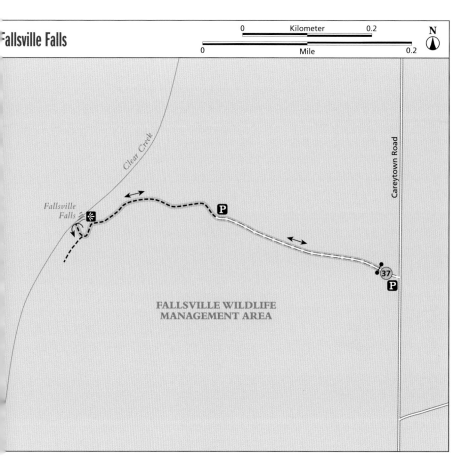

0.3 After passing a number of social trails on the right, arrive at a side trail on the right down to the water, marked with an old sign nailed to a tree that reads "W3." Take the trail down to the water, just below the falls. Return the way you came.

0.6 Arrive back at the trailhead.

Hike Information

Local information: Visitors Bureau of Highland County; (937) 393-1111; visithigh landcounty.com

38 Miller Falls

Come to Miller Nature Sanctuary for the spring wildflowers and stay for the waterfalls. April brings flowers you won't see everywhere, including shooting star and wild columbine, in addition to springtime classics like trillium, bluebell, and trout lily. Spring also brings a higher flow to these typically low-flow falls. Hike over cascading falls and then past the plunging Miller Falls. Parallel the Rocky Fork Creek, complete with riffling water, dense forest, and limestone cliffs. Finally, add in a couple of small natural bridges to complete this unique hike.

Height of falls: 5 feet; 15 feet
Type of falls: Cascade; plunge; ephemeral
Distance: 2.2-mile trail system
Difficulty: Easy
Hiking time: About 1 hour
Trail names: Miller Trail, Falls Trail, Arch Trail, connector trail
Trail surface: Gravel, dirt

Seasons and hours: Best mid-Apr; open daily, half hour before sunrise to half hour after sunset
Canine compatibility: Dogs not permitted
Trailhead facilities: None
Trail contact: Miller Nature Sanctuary State Nature Preserve; (740) 285-5971; ohiodnr .gov/go-and-do/plan-a-visit/find-a-property/ miller-nature-sanctuary-state-nature-preserve

Finding the trailhead: From US 50 in Rainsboro, turn south onto Barrett Mill Road and travel 2.2 miles to the preserve entrance on the left. It's before you cross Rocky Fork Creek. There is a parking lot next to the road. GPS: N39 12.06' / W83 23.36'

The Hike

Miller Nature Sanctuary State Nature Preserve punches above its weight when it comes to the size-to-scenery ratio. Dense spring wildflowers, the swiftly moving Rocky Fork Creek, natural bridges, and of course waterfalls make this 85-acre plot a worthwhile hiking destination. And there are even more trails nearby at Highlands Nature Sanctuary to check out while you're here.

Beginning at a parking lot just off Barrett Mill Road, walk past a gate along a 0.5-mile gravel service road to access the singletrack trails. Walk along the gravel road to a kiosk by the overlook for the arch, a small natural bridge composed of the easily soluble limestone-type rock known as Peebles Dolomite. Continue ahead on the connector trail to the Falls Trail and you'll soon hear a waterfall. This small but attractive waterfall is along a riffling, unnamed stream that flows into the Rocky Fork. There is a side trail to a bench for viewing the falls. In April look for shooting stars, trilliums, and other wildflowers at this spot.

On the way to the falls, if you look closely you'll also see cultivated flowers from the time when this was the homesite of Eugene and Henrietta Miller, who

Upper Falls at Miller Nature Sanctuary

transferred the property to the state in the 1980s. The trail takes you over the top of the small waterfall on a footbridge; this waterfall is alternately unnamed or referred to as Upper Falls or Henrietta Falls. Be sure to look upstream here as well; it is a very attractive spot. Continue hiking north, ascending gently to the ridgetop. When the trail descends on wooden steps back into the river valley, you'll pass a second, larger, arch. Look in the drainage for another ephemeral waterfall here. The trail then curves around to the south, and you will begin paralleling the Rocky Fork while walking upstream. Spring wildflowers are dense here and include Virginia bluebell, miter-wort/bishop's cap, hepatica, Dutchman's breeches, trout lily, and more. The botanical

Miller Falls

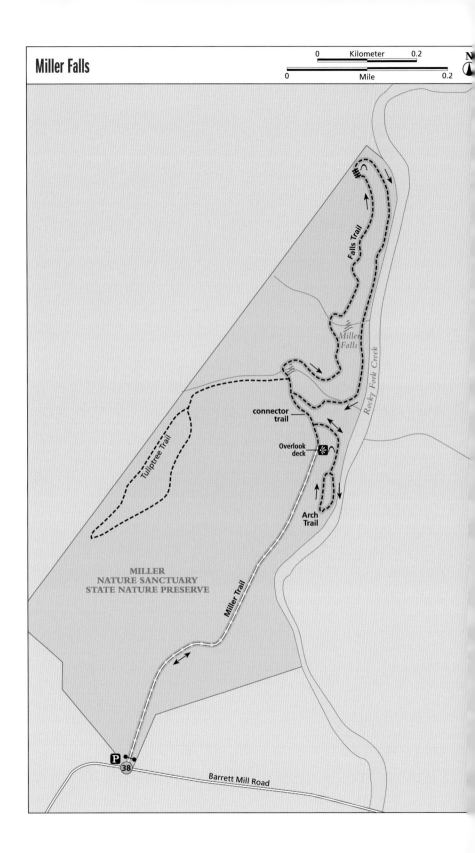

Falls Trail

Rocky Fork Creek

Miller Falls

Tuliptree Trail

connector trail

Overlook deck

Arch Trail

Miller Trail

MILLER
NATURE SANCTUARY
STATE NATURE PRESERVE

P
38

Barrett Mill Road

diversity here is due to the fact that it's at the edge of several physiographic regions. Southeast of here is Ohio's Appalachian region, unglaciated with a sandstone bedrock, while north and west of here is Ohio's Till Plains, left by the last glacier. South of here is a portion of the Kentucky Bluegrass region that juts into Ohio.

Walk by Miller Falls, pouring over a rock face on the unnamed stream shortly before it joins the Rocky Fork. On the way back to the trailhead, be sure to add the Arch Trail, which takes you to another view of the small arch, past slump blocks and through yet more wildflowers, still within view of the Rocky Fork, a swiftly moving Class I–II creek hemmed in by dolomite limestone walls. Downstream from here is the Rocky Fork Gorge, with walls up to 100 feet tall. While you're in the area, it's worth a visit to Highlands Nature Sanctuary to visit this feature spring through fall, when trails are open.

Miles and Directions

0.0 Start at the parking lot along Barrett Mill Road. Walk past the gate and follow the gravel service road north to a second, decommissioned parking area. (This service road is also known as the Miller Trail.) From here, continue north on a trail, passing another gate.

0.5 Pass a viewing platform on the right that overlooks a small arch. Then come to a junction with the Arch Trail on the right. Trend left onto the connector trail.

0.6 Pass the Tuliptree Trail on the left and continue straight. You will soon see and hear Upper Falls. You can take a short spur to a bench where you can view the falls and then return to the trail. From here, cross the stream on a wooden footbridge.

1.1 Take wooden stairs down into the creek valley and curve around to the right, paralleling the Rocky Fork upstream.

1.3 Cross a footbridge. To your right is the more-ephemeral Miller Falls.

1.4 Arrive back at the junction near the waterfall. Turn left.

1.5 Come to the junction with the Arch Trail. This time, take a left and complete the 0.2-mile lollipop that is the Arch Trail.

1.7 Arrive back at the connector trail. Take a left and return the way you came.

2.2 Arrive back at the parking lot by Barrett Mill Road.

Hike Information

Local information: Visitors Bureau of Highland County; (937) 393-1111; visithighlandcounty.com

Camping: Paint Creek State Park campground; (866) 644-6727; ohiodnr.gov/go-and-do/plan-a-visit/find-a-property/paint-creek-state-park-campground

39 Quiverheart Falls

Start with the quality that defines most Arc of Appalachia preserves—exceptionally outstanding spring wildflowers—then add a 15-foot waterfall, and you've got Quiverheart Gorge Preserve and its namesake waterfall. The preserve opened to the public in 2023; plan to return to this special place again and again as it continues to develop.

Height of falls: About 15 feet
Type of falls: Cascade to plunge
Distance: 1.9-mile lollipop
Difficulty: Moderate due to a few steep sections plus a stream crossing
Hiking time: About 1 hour
Trail name: Quiverheart Falls Trail
Trail surface: Dirt
Seasons and hours: Best in Apr; open daily, dawn to dusk

Canine compatibility: Dogs not permitted
Trailhead facilities: None
Trail contact: Arc of Appalachia Quiverheart Gorge Preserve; (937) 365-1935; arcof appalachia.org
Special considerations: This property is still under development. Be sure to check the website or Facebook page for updates.

Finding the trailhead: From SR 32, 1.2 miles east of Peebles, turn south onto Steam Furnace Road. Go 2.1 miles to a stop sign, where you join SR 781. Continue straight 0.1 mile to the preserve entrance and gravel parking lot on the right. GPS: N38 54.25' / W82 24.30'

The Hike

From the parking lot off Steam Furnace Road, Quiverheart Gorge Preserve is unassuming. Its farming and industrial past—a steam-powered iron blast furnace operated at this site in the 1800s—took a toll on the land. Hike past a mowed field on the Quiverheart Falls Trail into a young forest, where you will see old piles of charcoal and invasive plant species. In just a few minutes you'll arrive at Bundle Run and Quiverheart Falls. The falls are a once-hidden treasure now accessible to the general public.

Bundle Run serves as somewhat of a portal. As you hike out of the valley on the other side, you'll encounter an entirely different world of dolomite limestone cliffs covered in wildflowers like wood columbine, Solomon's seal, wood betony, and jack-in-the-pulpit. Along the ridgetop, cedar trees are common, and you'll be able to see more wildflowers, like hoary puccoon. A couple of rock outcroppings allow for overlooks of Bundle Run and Quiverheart Gorge.

Descend back into the gorge in between limestone cliffs and enter Boulder City, a portion of the property dotted with large boulders that double as spring wildflower nurseries. You'll find the boulders covered in trillium, miterwort, bloodroot, and more. Where you cross Bundle Run, the forest floor is covered in ramps (wild

Quiverheart Falls

leeks), phlox, and blue cohosh. Finish the loop by hiking upstream along Bundle Run under a rock overhang, where you can view a second, cascading waterfall. Look for the reddish color in the rock to see the iron content that was once mined here.

This property had been in the Baker family since 1965. The family developed the land into a horse farm and named it Quiverheart because the youngest family member, Matthew, said the horses made his heart quiver. Tragically, Matthew died in a car accident in 2002. The Baker family decided to create a nature preserve in Matthew's honor. The Bakers worked with the Arc of Appalachia preserve system to make the preserve a reality.

Miles and Directions

0.0 Start at the northern end of the parking lot and follow the trail from the meadow into the woods.

0.2 Come to a junction and turn right, descending into the gorge. Cross a metal footbridge where you can view Quiverheart Falls. Then ascend out of the gorge again via more stairs.

0.6 Come to a small overlook.

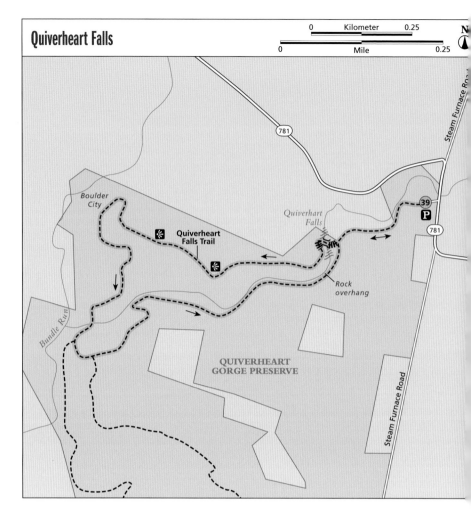

0.7 Arrive at a fork to a second overlook about 25 feet to the left. After checking out the view, return to the main trail and continue straight in the direction you were headed before the spur.

0.8 The trail turns left and descends through two limestone boulders.

1.1 Cross the creek. There is no footbridge here.

1.5 A trail joins from the right. Continue straight.

1.7 Walk under a rock overhang. Look for a cascading waterfall in the run.

1.75 Return to the first junction, where you descended into the gorge. This time, go straight.

1.9 Arrive back at the trailhead.

Hike Information

Local information: Adams County Travel & Visitors Bureau; (877) ADAMS-OH (877-232-6764); adamscountytravel.org

40 Cedar Falls, Edge of Appalachia Preserve

As the saying goes, it's not the destination, it's the journey. In the case of Cedar Falls in The Nature Conservancy's Edge of Appalachia Cedar Falls Preserve, it's really both. Hike a well-built trail over babbling runs, through a boulder field, and past A-list wildflowers to your final destination—Cedar Falls, a tiered waterfall on Cedar Run. Look and listen for more falls downstream as you approach.

Height of falls: 15 feet
Type of falls: Tiered
Distance: 3.4 miles out and back
Difficulty: Moderate due to length and elevation change
Hiking time: About 2 hours
Trail name: Helen C. Black Trail
Trail surface: Dirt

Seasons and hours: Best mid-Apr; open daily, dawn to dusk
Canine compatibility: Dogs not permitted
Trailhead facilities: None
Trail contact: Edge of Appalachia Preserve; (937) 544-2880; nature.org/en-us/get-involved/how-to-help/places-we-protect/edge-of-appalachia-cedar-falls-trail/

Finding the trailhead: From US 32 in Peebles, turn south on Steam Furnace Road. Go 5.1 miles to a stop sign at Fawcett Road. (***Note:*** SR 781 joins and then leaves Steam Furnace Road; watch closely to continue straight/south on Steam Furnace Road the entire way.) At the stop sign, turn left (east) onto White Oak Road (Fawcett Road goes west from here). In 0.2 mile you'll come to a fork where White Oak Road continues left; take the right fork onto Cedar Mills Road and continue 3.2 miles to the parking lot for Cedar Falls on the left, marked with a sign. GPS: N38 49.26' / W83 23.34'

The Hike

This is one of the newest waterfall hikes in Ohio; the trail was built and opened to the public in 2020. Named the Helen C. Black Trail, in memory of one of the preserve's most steadfast supporters, it is in the John and Marion Becker Cedar Falls Preserve, which in turn is part of The Nature Conservancy's Edge of Appalachia Preserve System. When you arrive, you'll see this area is like no other place in Ohio. Forests, prairies, and edge areas provide a dizzying array of flora and fauna. The hike to Cedar Falls will give you a nice sampling.

Cedar Run, a tributary that flows into Ohio Brush Creek, cuts a gorge as deep as 70 feet through the surrounding landscape, a geology composed mostly of dolomite limestone. Mid-April is a great time to visit, in part because the deciduous forest hasn't yet leafed out, allowing views of Cedar Run from the ridgetop. The green you see in the forest this time of year is the namesake cedars—eastern red cedars and northern white cedars, the latter of which are globally rare. Rare animal species

Cedar Falls, John and Marion Becker Cedar Falls Preserve

include the Allegheny wood rat, but you're more likely to enjoy the common animals that call this place home, including several species of woodpeckers and warblers, plus swallowtail and other butterflies.

The real gem of this preserve may be the waterfall, or it may be the dense spring wildflowers, including hepatica, trout lily, wild ginger, golden ragwort, and many more. As you walk through the boulder field in the spring, note how the boulders themselves provide a home to showy wildflowers like different species of trillium and miterwort, aka bishop's cap.

From the overlook, notice the waterfall and its more recent geologic history. The dolomite at the top of the falls is more resistant to the flow of water than the softer shale below, creating the waterfall. Note the large boulder lying in the streambed below the waterfall—that's a section of what was once the lip of the waterfall, which fell as the shale continued to erode and the waterfall "migrated" upstream.

If you aren't able to visit mid-April, when the spring wildflowers are at their peak, try to hike this trail in spring or winter, when the water will be flowing, or after a rain otherwise. The falls can slow down to a trickle in summer and fall.

Miles and Directions

0.0 Start at the trailhead kiosk on the east side of the parking lot. Walk north along the well-maintained trail. Within 0.3 mile, you'll cross two footbridges.

1.0 Walk through the boulder field.

1.7 Arrive at the end of the trail and a platform overlooking Cedar Falls. Retrace your steps to the trailhead.

3.4 Arrive back at the trailhead.

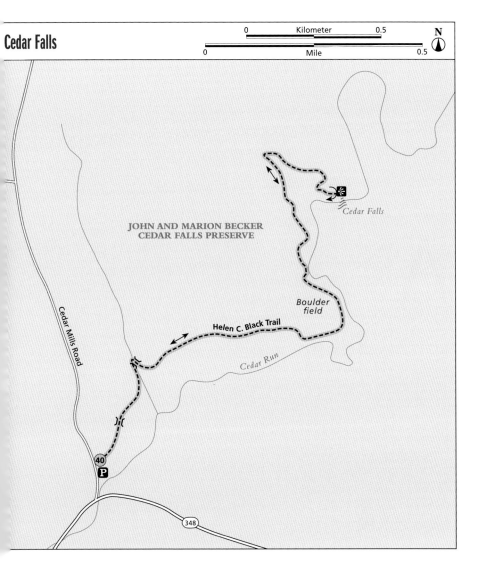

Hike Information

Local information: Adams County Travel & Visitors Bureau; (877) ADAMS-OH (877-232-6764); adamscountytravel.org

Southeast Ohio

Although there are a few outliers, most of southeast Ohio's waterfalls are concentrated in the Hocking Hills region—a region known specifically for its waterfalls (as well as its gorges and caves). These are all along creeks that cut the sandstone bedrock in hemlock-filled hollows. Many pour over sizable and impressive recess caves, like Ash Cave and Whispering Cave.

The last glacier did not reach into southeast Ohio, so the landscape here is hillier and more rugged than most of the rest of the state. Some of the waterways were influenced by the glacier, however, in the form of glacial runoff.

Hocking Hills State Park, home to Upper and Lower Falls (hike 46), Cedar Falls (hike 48), and Ash Cave Falls (hike 49), is extremely popular. Expect crowds, especially on weekends and during the summer, at these most popular sites. But even within the Hocking Hills region there are less-crowded hikes like Rockbridge State Nature Preserve (hike 43) and Big Spring Hollow Waterfall in Hocking State Forest (hike 45). The further afield you go, the more seclusion you can get on a waterfall hike.

Hocking Hills (explorehockinghills.com) is a great destination for waterfall hiking. Whether you go for a day or a week, there is enough to keep you busy. Plenty of trails, waterfalls, lodging, and other outdoor activities are concentrated in one area. Be sure to check out Ohio's newest state park lodge while you're there, whether to stay overnight or for a meal or a drink.

41 Rock Run Falls/Lake Katharine Spillway

Is it a natural waterfall? Well, Lake Katharine is not a natural lake—it was created by damming Rock Run. But the spillway used for the dam follows a natural, rocky streambed that leads to a cascade. The result? A beautiful waterfall in a preserve known for its bigleaf and umbrella magnolias. Spring brings flowing water and flowering trees.

Height of falls: About 18 feet
Type of falls: Cascade
Distance: 3.6-mile lollipop
Difficulty: Moderate due to length and hills
Hiking time: About 2 hours
Trail surface: Dirt
Trail names: Calico Bush Trail, Pine Ridge Trail
Seasons and hours: Best in May and June; open daily, half hour before sunrise to half hour after sunset

Canine compatibility: Dogs not permitted
Trailhead facilities: None
Trail contact: Lake Katharine State Nature Preserve; (740) 286-2487; ohiodnr.gov/go -and-do/plan-a-visit/find-a-property/lake -katharine-state-nature-preserve
Special considerations: Hiking off-trail is not allowed; this includes at the waterfall.

Finding the trailhead: From SR 93 on the north side of Jackson, turn west on Bridge Street (SR 93 turns to the east). Stay to the right where the road curves and Bridge Street becomes State Street. In about 1.5 miles you will cross two sets of railroad tracks. Just past the second set of tracks, turn right onto Lake Katharine Road, marked by a brown sign. Follow the road 2 miles to the parking area. GPS: N39 5.17' / W82 40.17'

The Hike

Lake Katharine is known to some as home to the northernmost patch of umbrella leaf and bigleaf magnolia trees in the country, and to be sure, it's worth a visit in the spring for that. But Lake Katharine is known to others as a place to hike to a waterfall—one of the few trailside waterfalls in southeast Ohio outside of the Hocking Hills.

Plan a visit in May or June to view the magnolias in bloom. Spring brings plenty of other flowers too. In April look for showy wildflowers like trillium, Dutchman's breeches, trout lily, and phlox. Lake Katharine is also home to some orchids as well, including rattlesnake plantain, whose leaves have a pattern resembling rattlesnake skin. Bonus: The leaves are evergreen, so you can see them year-round along the trail near the waterfall.

Start on the Calico Bush Trail; calico bush is another name for mountain laurel—another flowering plant found here at Lake Katharine, in this case, a shrub. Then you'll join the Pine Ridge Trail. Walk across the earthen dam and to the waterfall. Although there are Virginia pines on the preserve, the evergreens surrounding the waterfall are hemlock trees. Continue hiking on an upland trail where you will get views of Sharon Conglomerate rock outcroppings.

Rock Run Falls / Lake
Katharine Spillway

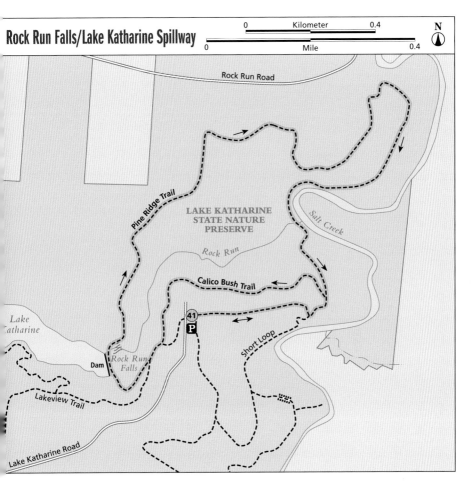

Linking the Calico Bush and Pine Ridge trails makes for a nice 3.6-mile loop. But there are several other miles of trail to explore at Lake Katharine, including the Lakeview Trail, which was constructed in 2020. While planning your visit, check the website for naturalist programming. Spring wildflower hikes are offered, and sometimes the manager offers off-trail waterfall hikes. When you return home, be sure to do a tick check, as ticks are common here.

Miles and Directions

0.0   Start the hike next to the parking lot at the trailhead sign listing all three trails, including the Pine Ridge Trail, which you begin here.

0.3   Come to a junction with the Salt Creek Trail. Turn left and then come to a second junction in quick succession for the Calico Bush Trail. Take another left and begin the Calico Bush Trail.

◀ *Rock Run Falls/Lake Katharine Spillway*

Rock Run Falls/Lake Katharine Spillway

0.9 Arrive at the junction where the Calico Bush Trail ends and the Pine Ridge Trail begins. Continue straight.

1.1 Cross the earthen dam and arrive at the Lake Katharine Spillway/Rock Run Falls.

3.3 Arrive back at the staggered junction with the Calico Bush Trail. Continue straight and come to the junction with the Salt Creek Trail. Keep right and retrace your steps from here to the parking lot and trailhead.

3.6 Arrive back at the trailhead.

Hike Information

Local information: City of Jackson Visitors & Conventions Commission; tourjackson ohio.com

Organizations: Friends of Lake Katharine; (740) 286-8054; friendsoflk.com

42 Rock Stalls Waterfall

Privately owned Rock Stalls Preserve has the classic components of a Hocking Hills destination: a cool gorge surrounded by hemlock trees and sandstone rock outcroppings, plus a beautiful waterfall. Not only is this a great alternative to the crowded hikes in Hocking Hills State Park, it's also a uniquely situated waterfall, pouring over a right angle where two sandstone walls meet.

Height of falls: About 15 feet
Type of falls: Plunge
Distance: 1.3-mile trail system
Difficulty: Moderate due to stream crossing and steepness
Hiking time: About 45 minutes
Trail name: Trail is unnamed.
Trail surface: Dirt
Seasons and hours: Best in spring; open daily, 9 a.m. to 5 p.m.

Canine compatibility: Not posted, assume that dogs are not permitted.
Trailhead facilities: None
Trail contact: Camp Akita; (614) 488-0681; campakita.org
Special considerations: Note the many variations on the Rock Stalls name: Rockstall, Rock Stull, etc. Follow the directions here, and you will find the waterfall.

Finding the trailhead: From US 33 in Logan, take SR 664 North for 5.6 miles to Logan Horns Mill Road. Turn left and go 2 miles to a three-way intersection with Rock Stull Road. Turn right and continue 0.4 mile (past the Rock Stalls House) to the parking on the right, marked with a "Rockstall Nature Preserve" sign.

The Hike

The Hocking Hills region is known for its waterfalls. Not surprisingly, there are plenty of falls in the region that are outside of Hocking Hills State Park. Case in point: the lovely waterfall at Rock Stalls, which is owned and operated by Camp Akita, a summer camp operated by the First Community Church in Columbus.

Separated from the rest of the camp by Rock Stull Road, Rock Stalls has its own trailhead parking for the general public. Walk in a young forest, which is primarily composed of beech and maple trees. It's a good idea to wear pants for this hike because of the trailside multiflora rose and stinging nettles you'll encounter. But there is plenty of beauty in this forest as well. Spring wildflowers include trillium and trout lily. Listen for the songs of vireos, thrushes, and woodpeckers.

Hike down toward the stream, which requires a crossing with no footbridge. The waterfall is relatively low flow, so plan to come when it has been raining. Which means, plan to wear waterproof boots. Stepping stones aid the creek crossing. On the other side of the creek, come to a long sandstone rock wall. Follow it upstream until you get to the falls at a unique spot where two sandstone walls meet, forming

Rock Stalls waterfall

a nearly perfect right angle. In high water, look and listen for more ephemeral falls nearby. On the return trip, cross the creek again and then complete the loop trail on the other side.

Another waterfall that is quite nearby is Robinson Falls, also known as Corkscrew Falls. It is on nearby Boch Hollow State Nature Preserve land. These waterfalls are accessible by permit only, but the permit is free and easy to get by contacting the Ohio Department of Nature Resources Division of Natural Areas and Preserves.

Miles and Directions

0.0 Start at the gate on the north end of the gravel parking lot. Walk into the woods. In about 250 feet, come to a junction with a trail on the right. There is a sign here for Rock Stalls. Continue straight.

0.5 Come to stairs and descend them. About halfway down is a trail on the right. Continue straight. At the bottom of the stairs, cross the creek on stepping stones. Then walk upstream, paralleling the creek. Stay at the bottom of the sandstone rock outcroppings.

0.7 Arrive at the Rock Stalls waterfall. Turn around and retrace your steps to the stairs.

0.8 Halfway up the stairs, take the side trail this time, to the left.

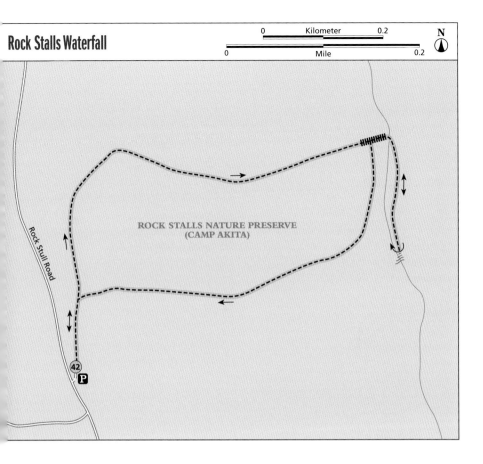

1.2 Return to the first junction, at the "Rock Stalls" sign. Turn left and walk back to the trailhead.

1.3 Arrive back at the parking lot.

Hike Information

Local information: Hocking Hills Tourism Association; (800) HOCKING (800-462-5464), (740) 385-9706; explorehockinghills.com

Camping: Hocking Hills State Park Campground; (866) 644-6727; ohiodnr.gov/go -and-do/plan-a-visit/find-a-property/hocking-hills-state-park-campground

Lodging: Hocking Hills State Park Lodge; (800) AT-A-PARK (800-282-7275); ohiodnr.gov/go-and-do/plan-a-visit/find-a-property/hocking-hills-lodge -conference-center

43 Rockbridge Falls

This uniquely situated waterfall plunges over the lip of a recess cave adjacent to the state's longest natural rock bridge, nearly 100 feet long. Enjoy a hike through fields and forest, past rock features, to the waterfall and rock bridge, and then to the edge of the Hocking River.

Height of falls: 50 feet
Type of falls: Cave
Distance: 2.8-mile trail system
Difficulty: Moderate due to some rough trail and steep sections
Hiking time: About 1 hour
Trail names: Bridge Trail, Rock Shelter Trail, Canoe Access Trail
Trail surface: Dirt

Seasons and hours: Best late fall through early spring; open daily, half hour before sunrise to half hour after sunset
Canine compatibility: Dogs not permitted
Trailhead facilities: None
Trail contact: Rockbridge State Nature Preserve; (740) 380-8919; ohiodnr.gov/go-and-do/plan-a-visit/find-a-property/rockbridge-state-nature-preserve

Finding the trailhead: From US 33 between Rockbridge and Logan just east of the rest area, turn north onto Dalton Road—there is a brown road sign here for Rockbridge State Nature Preserve. Take an immediate right and follow signs 0.7 mile through a sharp left turn to the parking area on the left. GPS: N39 33.59' / W82 29.57'

The Hike

This unique and attractive waterfall is best in spring, as it is generally a low-flow waterfall. But this trail system is otherwise worth visiting any time of year for Ohio's longest natural sandstone bridge. Begin on the Bridge Trail (formerly named Natural Bridge Trail) by walking along a farm field, paralleling the fence line where there is a strip of trees. Look and listen for meadow birds here like bobolinks, bluebirds, and eastern meadowlarks. In about 0.5 mile the trail enters the woods, a mostly maple-beech forest but with a wide variety of tree species.

Come to a signed intersection for both the Bridge (blazed orange) and Rock Shelter (blazed blue) trails. Most people choose to hike only the Bridge Trail, but it's worthwhile to hike the Rock Shelter Trail. It will take you past a recess cave and an ephemeral waterfall. Early spring—before the leaves have come out—is a great time to see both the rock features and water flowing. Alternately, late fall, when the beech leaves are still yellow but most other leaves have fallen, is also a good time to see rock features. It's best to go after a rain in the fall.

The Bridge Trail takes you to the namesake sandstone arch, nearly 100 feet across. You are able to walk across the narrow bridge and back, then down underneath, where you'll get the best view of the waterfall. Stay on the designated trail. The

Rockbridge Falls

Hocking Hills Region in one respect is anchored by the Hocking River, but this is the only substantial trail on public land that takes you right to the river's edge. From the falls, take the short Canoe Access Trail to the river. It's a good spot for skipping rocks, eating lunch, and quite possibly seeing boaters pull up their rigs to take a side trip to the rock bridge.

Miles and Directions

0.0 Start at the trailhead kiosk at the small parking lot. Hike on a wide, clear path that parallels the fence line.

0.5 Pass a trail on the left and continue straight.

0.6 Arrive at a signed junction and turn right to hike the Rock Shelter Trail. (**Option:** For a shorter hike, cut out the Rock Shelter Trail and turn left here to go directly to the rock bridge.)

1.0 Come to a junction for a loop trail. Hike the loop in either direction and return to this spot.

1.2 Return to the beginning of the loop and retrace your steps back to the signed junction.

1.6 Arrive back at the signed junction; this time continue straight on the Bridge Trail.

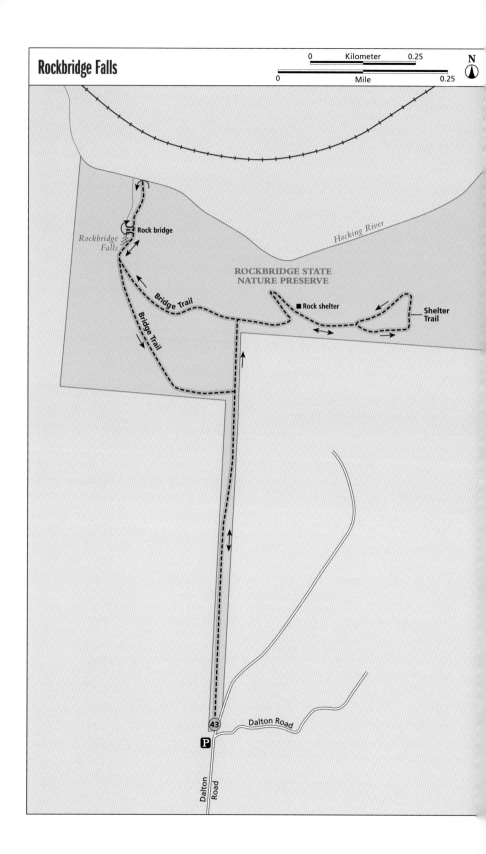

Rockbridge Falls

0   Kilometer   0.25

0   Mile   0.25

N

Rock bridge

Rockbridge Falls

Hocking River

ROCKBRIDGE STATE NATURE PRESERVE

■ Rock shelter

Shelter Trail

Bridge Trail

Bridge Trail

43

P

Dalton Road

Dalton Road

Rockbridge Falls

1.8 Come to a junction marked with a post. Turn right and hike to the rock bridge and water-fall. After checking out the falls and the rock bridge, continue past them, walking north to the banks of the Hocking River.

1.9 Arrive at the Hocking River. Turn around and retrace your steps past the rock bridge and waterfall to the junction marked with a post.

2.0 At the junction marked with a post, turn right.

2.3 Come to a T intersection with the trail where you started. Turn right and retrace your steps to the trailhead and parking.

2.8 Arrive back at the trailhead.

Hike Information

Local information: Hocking Hills Tourism Association; (800) HOCKING (800-462-5464), (740) 385-9706; explorehockinghills.com

Camping: Hocking Hills State Park Campground; (866) 644-6727; ohiodnr.gov/go-and-do/plan-a-visit/find-a-property/hocking-hills-state-park-campground

Lodging: Hocking Hills State Park Lodge; (800) AT-A-PARK (800-282-7275); ohiodnr.gov/go-and-do/plan-a-visit/find-a-property/hocking-hills-lodge-conference-center

44 Lower Falls, Conkles Hollow State Nature Preserve

Conkles Hollow is a popular Hocking Hills destination, providing some of the best vistas in the state, as seen from the Rim Trail. But the Gorge Trail is spectacular in its own right, with sandstone cliffs rising up to 200 feet on either side, abundant spring wildflowers, and, to top it all off, a waterfall at the head of the gorge, hemmed in tightly by cliffs and pouring into a small pool.

Height of falls: About 12 feet
Type of falls: Plunge
Distance: 3.2-mile trail system; optional 1.2 miles out and back to the waterfall
Difficulty: Moderate to difficult due to steep steps out of the gorge
Hiking time: About 1.5 hours
Trail names: Rim Trail, Gorge Trail
Trail surface: Dirt, concrete
Seasons and hours: Best in spring; open daily, half hour before sunrise to half hour after sunset

Canine compatibility: Dogs not permitted
Trailhead facilities: Restrooms, picnic tables
Trail contact: Conkles Hollow State Nature Preserve; (740) 380-8919; ohiodnr.gov/ go-and-do/plan-a-visit/find-a-property/ conkles-hollow-state-nature-preserve
Special considerations: This is an extremely popular hike, so consider visiting on a weekday. Please use extreme caution when hiking the Rim Trail, as the cliff edges are dangerous; a number of fatalities have occurred due to off-trail activity.

Finding the trailhead: From US 33 in Logan, turn south on SR 664 and drive 12 miles (passing Old Man's Cave and the visitor center) to SR 374. Turn right (north) and travel 1 mile to Big Pine Road. Turn right again and continue 0.2 mile to the parking lot on the left. The trailhead is on the far end cul-de-sac in the parking lot, where it meets the woods and the creek. GPS: N39 27.2' / W82 34.23'

The Hike

Whether you're looking for vistas, wildflowers, or waterfalls, Conkles Hollow has it for you. This is one of the most popular hikes in the state, and it deserves to be. Begin by crossing Pine Creek and then ascend out of the hollow on some calf-burning steps. This is the Rim Trail, marked with red blazes. Hike in a mixed hardwood and evergreen forest. Hemlocks and Virginia pines help make this a beautiful hike year-round. From the Rim Trail, stop at a series of vistas—something unusual in Ohio. You can see several ridges undulate to the horizon.

As you approach the head of the hollow, there is a wooden observation deck for the waterfall. The forest is too thick here to see the waterfall, but you can hear it and otherwise get a view of the hollow. Then cross over the unnamed tributary to Pine Creek that creates the waterfall before finishing the loop on the other side of the hollow.

ower Falls at Conkles Hollow, more commonly known as Conkles Hollow Falls

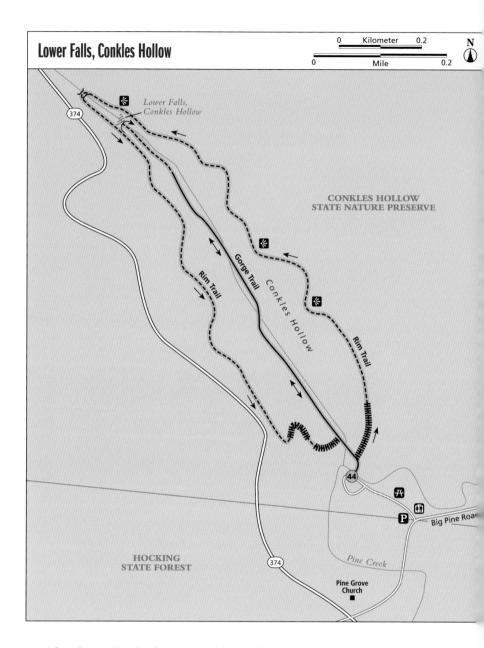

0   Kilometer   0.2

0   Mile   0.2

N

CONKLES HOLLOW
STATE NATURE PRESERVE

Lower Falls,
Conkles Hollow

374

Rim Trail

Gorge Trail

Conkles Hollow

Rim Trail

44

Big Pine Road

P

HOCKING
STATE FOREST

374

Pine Creek

Pine Grove
Church

After descending back into Conkles Hollow, join the concrete, ADA-accessible trail into the hollow. (The wheelchair-accessible trail ends before a view of the water-fall.) This is the Gorge Trail, which has a green blaze. Spring wildflowers here are abundant, including trillium, Dutchman's breeches, trout lily, and Virginia bluebell. The hollow is narrow, only 100–300 feet wide, and as you continue upstream, the Blackhand Sandstone walls tower up to 200 feet above. End at the waterfall, which plunges into a small pool. The waterfall is quite nice but can have low flow. So plan to go in the spring and, even better, after a rain. This is called Lower Falls; Middle Falls is obscured, and Upper Falls is what you hear from the overlook platform.

Planning ahead is important if you have pets. Pets are not allowed at Conkles Hollow because it is a state nature preserve primarily dedicated to habitat preservation instead of recreation. Dogs can stomp flora and stress fauna. So either leave your best friend at home or plan to hike at nearby Hocking Hills State Park or Hocking State Forest.

Miles and Directions

0.0 Start at the trailhead by the cul-de-sac. Cross a footbridge over Pine Creek, pass a trailhead kiosk, and arrive at wooden stairs.

0.1 Turn right and ascend the stairs out of the gorge. This is the Rim Trail, blazed red.

0.4 Come to the first of several sandstone outcropping overlooks.

1.0 Arrive at the wooden overlook above the waterfall.

1.1 Cross the creek on a footbridge. Return on the west side of the gorge, walking downstream.

2.1 After descending back into the hollow, reach the trailhead for the Gorge Trail. Turn left and walk upstream, following the green blazes.

2.6 Come to the end of the Gorge Trail, at the bottom of the falls.

3.1 Return to the Gorge Trail trailhead the way you came. Continue straight.

3.2 Arrive back at the trailhead.

Hike Information

Local information: Hocking Hills Tourism Association; (800) HOCKING (800-462-5464), (740) 385-9706; explorehockinghills.com
Camping: Hocking Hills State Park Campground; (866) 644-6727; ohiodnr.gov/go-and-do/plan-a-visit/find-a-property/hocking-hills-state-park-campground
Lodging: Hocking Hills State Park Lodge; (800) AT-A-PARK (800-282-7275); ohiodnr.gov/go-and-do/plan-a-visit/find-a-property/hocking-hills-lodge-conference-center

45 Big Spring Hollow Falls

The 120-foot waterfall at the head of Big Spring Hollow is not only the tallest known waterfall in the Buckeye State, it's also the only waterfall in Ohio where you might very well glimpse rappellers descending ropes alongside the falls. Hocking State Forest is less popular—that is, less crowded—than Hocking Hills State Park. But the hike through Big Spring Hollow showcases all of the things to love about the Hocking Hills region: waterfalls, caves, gorges, hemlocks, and wildflowers. This is generally a low-flow waterfall, but impressive nonetheless.

Height of falls: 120 feet
Type of falls: Plunge
Distance: 1.4 miles out and back
Difficulty: Easy
Hiking time: About 1 hour
Trail names: Buckeye Trail, unnamed trail
Trail surface: Dirt

Seasons and hours: Best winter and spring; open daily, sunrise to sunset
Canine compatibility: Controlled dogs permitted
Trailhead facilities: None
Trail contact: Hocking State Forest; (740) 385-4402; forestry.ohiodnr.gov/hocking

Finding the trailhead: From US 33 in Logan, go south on SR 664 for 3.9 miles to Big Pine Road. Take a right and continue 5.7 miles to the Hocking State Forest Rock Climbing and Rappelling Area parking on the right. From the parking lot, cross Big Pine Road and start at the "Hocking State Forest Rock Climbing and Rappelling Area" sign. GPS: N39 27.31' / W82 33.28'

The Hike

Hocking State Forest shares many of the same features as Hocking Hills State Park: waterfalls, caves, creeks, gorges, hemlocks. But the state forest has fewer restrictions than the state park, so a wider variety of outdoor enthusiasts congregates here, including horseback riders, rock climbers, and rappellers. Home to one of the few sanctioned rock climbing and rappelling areas in Ohio, Hocking State Forest is popular in part because it's possible to rappel alongside the waterfall at the head of Big Spring Hollow. If you hike to these falls on a warm weekend, there's a decent chance you'll see rappellers with your own eyes.

The trail to the falls begins across from the parking lot and starts along the 1,400-mile statewide Buckeye Trail. After crossing the footbridge over Pine Creek, however, the BT turns left where you take a right to start the hike to Big Spring Hollow. Horses share this trail, so it can get extremely muddy in the spring; be sure to bring appropriate footwear. Big Spring is named for a spring at the head of the hollow, but it could just as easily refer to how fantastic it is here in spring, where wildflowers carpet the forest floor. These include harbinger of spring, hepatica, trout lily, trillium, and more.

Spring Hollow Falls

Big Spring Hollow Falls

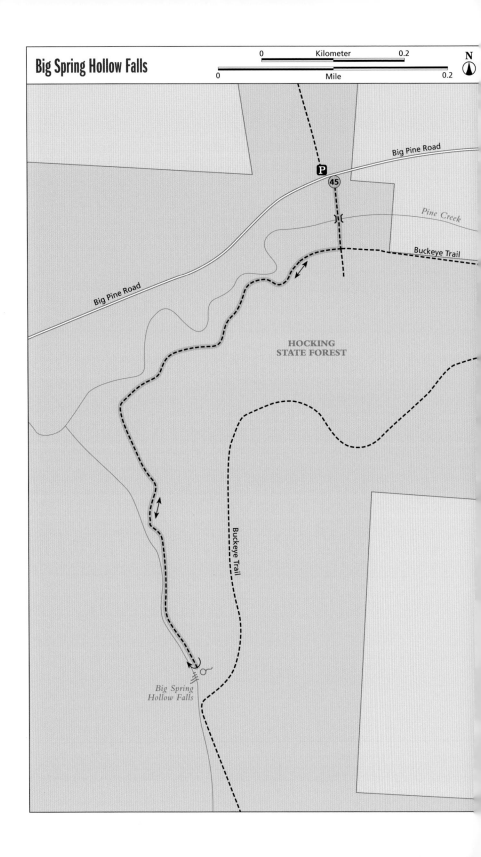

Big Spring Hollow Falls

0   Kilometer   0.2

0   Mile   0.2

N

Big Pine Road

P

45

Pine Creek

Buckeye Trail

Big Pine Road

HOCKING
STATE FOREST

Buckeye Trail

Big Spring
Hollow Falls

Rappelling alongside Big Spring Hollow Falls

The hollow narrows as you hike upstream, and rock walls come into view. You'll likely hear the waterfall before you see it. The waterfall is not sourced by the big spring, however. If you hike to the top of the ridge to the left (east) side of the waterfall, you can see where water discharges from the spring—in the springtime, the flow is quite impressive.

As long as you're in the area, it's worthwhile to check out a couple of nearby features. After crossing the footbridge, instead of heading right to Big Spring Hollow, take a left and follow the Buckeye Trail 0.5 mile to balanced rock. Alternatively, from the parking lot hike north on the horse trail past Chapel Cave and to the end of this hollow, where you can glimpse an ephemeral waterfall (Twin Falls) in the spring or after a good rain.

Miles and Directions

0.0 Start just off the side of Big Pine Road at the "Hocking State Forest Rock Climbing and Rappelling Area" sign. You'll see a blue blaze for the Buckeye Trail. Cross Pine Creek on a footbridge and come to a four-way intersection. Take a right and follow this unnamed trail to its end at the Big Spring Hollow Waterfall.

0.7 Arrive at the head of Big Spring Hollow and the waterfall. Turn around and retrace your steps to the trailhead.

1.4 Arrive back at the trailhead.

Hike Information

Local information: Hocking Hills Tourism Association; (800) HOCKING (800-462-5464), (740) 385-9706; explorehockinghills.com
Organizations: Buckeye Trail Association; (740) 394-2008; buckeyetrail.org
Camping: Hocking Hills State Park Campground; (866) 644-6727; ohiodnr.gov/go-and-do/plan-a-visit/find-a-property/hocking-hills-state-park-campground
Lodging: Hocking Hills State Park Lodge; (800) AT-A-PARK (800-282-7275); ohiodnr.gov/go-and-do/plan-a-visit/find-a-property/hocking-hills-lodge-conference-center

46 Upper and Lower Falls, Hocking Hills State Park

This is one of the most waterfall-intensive hikes in Ohio. In addition to the named falls—Upper Falls, Lower Falls, Broken Rock Falls—come after a rain and find numerous other unnamed, ephemeral falls. Old Man's Creek created this gorge, where water rushes year-round. The hike would be beautiful even without the falls, but the waterfalls are what make this one of the most popular and signature hikes in the Buckeye State.

Height of falls: 20 feet; 30 feet
Type of falls: Cascade to plunge
Distance: 2.0-mile loop
Difficulty: Moderate due to many steps
Hiking time: About 1 hour
Trail names: Grandma Gatewood/Buckeye Trail, Gorge Exit Trail
Trail surface: Dirt, stone
Seasons and hours: Good year-round, best on weekdays; open daily, half hour before sunrise to half hour after sunset

Canine compatibility: Dogs permitted on a 6-foot leash
Trailhead facilities: Visitor center, water, restrooms, picnic area
Trail contact: Hocking Hills State Park; (740) 385-6842; ohiodnr.gov/go-and-do/plan-a-visit/find-a-property/hocking-hills-state-park
Special considerations: This is an extremely popular hike; consider going on a weekday if possible. Swimming and wading are prohibited.

Finding the trailhead: From US 33 in Logan, turn south onto SR 664 and go 10.2 miles to the Old Man's Cave parking on the left. Near the eastern end of the parking lot (opposite side from the visitor center), take the steps down to the sidewalk. Turn left and walk to the trailhead kiosk. Across from the kiosk, a ramp begins the trail, marked with a "Trail Entrance" sign. GPS: N39 26.11' / W82 32.20'

The Hike

Start at the Upper Falls trailhead; you'll hear the falls before you even see them. As you walk across the bridge that takes you over the falls, look upstream to see your first waterfall, basically the upper portion of Upper Falls. You'll get your first good view of Upper Falls before you descend into the gorge, where you can approach the large pool the falls empty into.

Continue downstream, following the blue blazes of the Buckeye Trail. This section of the BT is also named the Grandma Gatewood Trail, in honor of Emma "Grandma" Gatewood, the first woman to solo thru-hike the Appalachian Trail. An Ohio native, she thru-hiked the AT in 1955, at age 67—and did it again after that! She was also a founding member of the Buckeye Trail Association.

Upper Falls

Continuing downstream you'll pass over Devil's Bathtub and walk along many features built by the Civilian Conservation Corps in the 1930s, including stone steps and a tunnel that leads to a view of Old Man's Cave across the creek. A smaller waterfall drops along the creek here. Since the COVID-19 pandemic, Hocking Hills State Park has maintained this section of trail as one way. This decision makes sense; millions traverse this trail each year, and this cuts down on congestion.

Downstream from Old Man's Cave is Lower Falls, another beautiful, year-round waterfall that plunges into a large pool. Exiting the BT after Lower Falls, be sure to take a short spur trail to Broken Rock Falls. This waterfall is along a side drainage to Old Man's Creek, so water does not flow year-round. But when the water is high, these falls are uniquely beautiful. The surrounding landscape could be described as primordial.

Take more stairs and another tunnel out of the gorge, finishing the hike at the visitor center. In fact, you might choose to begin the hike at the visitor center to learn more about the history, geology, flora, and fauna of the hike before setting out.

Lower Falls

Upper and Lower Falls; Whispering Cave Falls

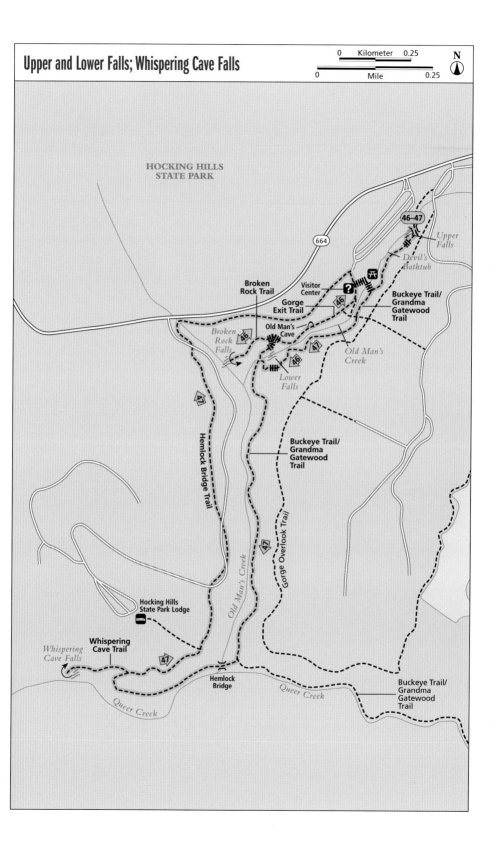

0   Kilometer   0.25

0   Mile   0.25

N

HOCKING HILLS
STATE PARK

664

46–47

*Upper
Falls*

*Devil's
Bathtub*

Broken
Rock Trail

Visitor
Center

?

Buckeye Trail/
Grandma
Gatewood
Trail

Gorge
Exit Trail

46

Old Man's
Cave

*Broken
Rock
Falls*

46

47

46

*Old Man's
Creek*

*Lower
Falls*

47

Buckeye Trail/
Grandma
Gatewood
Trail

Hemlock Bridge Trail

Gorge Overlook Trail

47

Old Man's Creek

Hocking Hills
State Park Lodge

Whispering
Cave Trail

*Whispering
Cave Falls*

47

Hemlock
Bridge

Queer Creek

Buckeye Trail/
Grandma
Gatewood
Trail

Queer Creek

Broken Rock Falls

Miles and Directions

0.0 Start at the Upper Falls trailhead kiosk and take the wooden ramp to the bridge that crosses over Upper Falls. Walk downstream to a set of steps that take you into the gorge. At the bottom of the steps, turn right to view Upper Falls. After viewing the falls, turn around and walk downstream on the Buckeye Trail.

0.2 Cross the creek at Devil's Bathtub.

0.3 Pass stone steps on the right that lead out of the gorge to the visitor center. Continue straight.

0.5 Walk through a tunnel. Across the creek is Old Man's Cave.

0.7 Come to a junction with a trail that crosses the creek on a stone bridge. This takes you to Old Man's Cave (and continues out of the gorge back to the visitor center). Instead of crossing the bridge, continue straight (downstream).

0.9 At a junction, the BT goes left, continuing downstream. Go right here and cross a stone bridge and walk to Lower Falls. To the left of the falls are steps that take you out of the gorge. Take these steps.

1.1 At the top of the steps, arrive at a T intersection. Turn left, following a sign for Broken Rock Falls. This is the Broken Rock Falls Trail.

1.2 Arrive at Broken Rock Falls. After the falls, turn back and retrace your steps to the last junction.

1.3 At the junction, continue straight this time and walk up a curving staircase. You are now on the Gorge Exit Trail.

1.5 Arrive at a stone tunnel. Take the stairs up through the tunnel and exit at the top of the gorge. Then walk a flat trail that parallels the creek upstream. Pass the naturalist cabin and the Gorge Overlook Trail on the right. Continue straight.

1.8 Pass the visitor center on the left. Continue on the sidewalk back to the trailhead or to your vehicle.

2.0 Arrive back at the trailhead.

Hike Information

Local information: Hocking Hills Tourism Association; (800) HOCKING (800-462-5464), (740) 385-9706; explorehockinghills.com

Organizations: Friends of Hocking Hills State Park; (877) 403-4477
Buckeye Trail Association; (740) 394-2008; buckeyetrail.org

Camping: Hocking Hills State Park Campground; (866) 644-6727; ohiodnr.gov/go-and-do/plan-a-visit/find-a-property/hocking-hills-state-park-campground

Lodging: Hocking Hills State Park Lodge; (800) AT-A-PARK (800-282-7275); ohiodnr.gov/go-and-do/plan-a-visit/find-a-property/hocking-hills-lodge-conference-center

Lower Falls in winter

47 Whispering Cave Falls

Whispering Cave Falls is the less popular—that is, less crowded—cousin to Ash Cave Falls. Enjoy a hike to these 100-foot falls plunging over the lip of a 300-foot-wide cave. As a bonus, you hike past some of the most popular and beautiful falls in the Hocking Hills on the way to this one. **(See map on page 201.)**

Height of falls: 100 feet
Type of falls: Cave
Distance: 4.25-mile loop (optional 1.2 miles out and back)
Difficulty: Moderate due to length and steps
Hiking time: About 2 hours
Trail names: Grandma Gatewood/Buckeye Trail, Hemlock Bridge Trail, Whispering Cave Trail
Trail surface: Dirt, stone

Seasons and hours: Good in winter and spring, best on weekdays; open daily, half hour before sunrise to half hour after sunset
Canine compatibility: Dogs permitted on a 6-foot leash
Trailhead facilities: Visitor center, water, restrooms, picnic area
Trail contact: Hocking Hills State Park; (740) 385-6842; ohiodnr.gov/go-and-do/plan-a-visit/find-a-property/hocking-hills-state-park

Finding the trailhead: From US 33 in Logan, turn south onto SR 664 and go 10.2 miles to the Old Man's Cave parking on the left. Near the eastern end of the parking lot (opposite side from the visitor center), take the steps down to the sidewalk. Turn left and walk to the trailhead kiosk. Across from the kiosk, a ramp begins the trail, marked with a "Trail Entrance" sign. GPS: N39 26.11' / W82 32.20'

The Hike

The hike to Whispering Cave is a perfect outing if you're looking for a loop that has more length than the most popular Hocking Hills hikes. The bonus is that you will hike by Upper Falls and Lower Falls on the way. Plan to come after a rain and you'll be rewarded with practically innumerable ephemeral falls while you're at it. Be sure to wear appropriate footwear, as the trail can get muddy in spots after a rain. (**Option:** For a shorter hike, begin at the Hocking Hills Lodge and walk directly to Whispering Cave and back for a 1.2-mile hike.)

It's worth stopping in at the visitor center to familiarize yourself with the Hocking Hills. From the visitor center, take a sidewalk to the opposite end of the parking lot. Starting at the Upper Falls trailhead kiosk, walk over the upper part of Upper Falls—look left to see your first cascade just steps after you enter the trail—and then walk into the gorge to view Upper Falls and the large pool it pours into. Then hike downstream along the Grandma Gatewood Trail—named for Emma "Grandma" Gatewood, the first woman to solo thru-hike the Appalachian Trail in 1955, at age 67, and a founding member of the Buckeye Trail Association.

Whispering Cave Falls

Enjoy the sandstone cliffs, hemlock forest, and rushing water as you make your way to a view across the creek of Old Man's Cave, named for a hermit who is said to have lived in the cave in the 1700s. Then continue to Lower Falls. After Lower Falls, the crowds drop off precipitously as you continue downstream on the Grandma Gatewood Trail, which doubles as the Buckeye Trail (BT) in the park. As the saying goes, follow the blue blazes.

When you arrive at the Hemlock Bridge Trail, exit the BT, walk over a "swinging" suspension bridge, and then continue to the Whispering Cave Trail, which takes you to the cave and back. Whispering Cave is so named for its acoustics. It looks very much like a smaller version of Ash Cave, but it's less crowded if solitude is what you're looking for. Finish the hike by completing a loop that takes you along the Hemlock Bridge Trail to a service road that ends at the visitor center.

Miles and Directions

0.0 Start at the Upper Falls trailhead kiosk and take the wooden ramp to the bridge that crosses over Upper Falls. Then walk downstream to a set of steps that take you into the gorge. At the bottom of the steps, turn right to view Upper Falls. After viewing the falls, turn around and walk downstream on the Buckeye Trail.

0.2 Cross the creek at Devil's Bathtub.

0.3 Pass stone steps on the right that lead out of the gorge to the visitor center. Continue straight.

0.5 Walk through a tunnel. Across the creek is Old Man's Cave.

0.7 Come to a junction with a trail that crosses the creek on a stone bridge. This takes you to Old Man's Cave (and continues out of the gorge back to the visitor center). Continue straight (downstream).

0.9 At a junction, the BT goes left and a stone bridge takes you over the creek to Lower Falls. After viewing Lower Falls, continue walking downstream, following the blue blazes.

1.8 Come to a fork. The BT goes left. Take a right onto the signed Hemlock Bridge Trail. Cross the bridge and continue.

2.2 Arrive at a T intersection. Take a left onto the Whispering Cave Trail.

2.4 Arrive at Whispering Cave Falls. Retrace your steps to the previous junction.

2.8 Return to the junction with the Hemlock Bridge Trail; continue straight.

3.0 Come to a four-way junction. To the left is the lodge; to the right is an overlook. Continue straight.

3.4 Cross the road and continue straight.

3.8 Cross the road again and join a paved trail/access road. Follow this all the way to the visitor center.

4.25 Arrive at the visitor center, by the parking lot.

Hike Information

Local information: Hocking Hills Tourism Association; (800) HOCKING (800-462-5464), (740) 385-9706; explorehockinghills.com

Organizations: Friends of Hocking Hills State Park; (877) 403-4477

Buckeye Trail Association; (740) 394-2008; buckeyetrail.org

Camping: Hocking Hills State Park Campground; (866) 644-6727; ohiodnr.gov/go-and-do/plan-a-visit/find-a-property/hocking-hills-state-park-campground

Lodging: Hocking Hills State Park Lodge; (800) AT-A-PARK (800-282-7275); ohiodnr.gov/go-and-do/plan-a-visit/find-a-property/hocking-hills-lodge-conference-center

Whispering Cave Falls

48 Cedar Falls, Hocking Hills State Park

Cedar Falls is arguably the most spectacular waterfall in a park known for its waterfalls. Take a short but steep hike to the highest-volume waterfall in the Hocking Hills, surrounded by cliffs and evergreen hemlock trees—Cedar Falls is a misnomer—and if you go at the right time, you'll be rewarded with a view of Hidden Falls as well.

Height of falls: 50 feet tall, 5 feet wide
Type of falls: Cascade to plunge
Distance: 0.6-mile loop
Difficulty: Moderate due to steep ascent out of the gorge
Hiking time: About 20 minutes
Trail names: Buckeye Trail, Cedar Falls Trail
Trail surface: Dirt

Best seasons: Best in spring and winter; open daily, half hour before sunrise to half hour after sunset
Canine compatibility: Dogs permitted on a 6-foot leash
Trailhead facilities: Water, restrooms, picnic area
Trail contact: Hocking Hills State Park; (740) 385-6842; ohiodnr.gov/go-and-do/plan-a-visit/find-a-property/hocking-hills-state-park

Finding the trailhead: From US 33 in Logan, turn south onto SR 664 and drive 8.2 miles to SR 374. Turn left and drive 1.8 miles to the Cedar Falls entrance on the left. The trailhead is at the second parking lot, the one farther from the road. GPS: N39 25.05' / W82 31.35'

The Hike

Cedar Falls is one of the most beloved hiking destinations in the state of Ohio. Good infrastructure, easy (though steep) access, and beautiful surroundings make this a bucket-list waterfall hike. Beginning at the Cedar Falls Trail kiosk, descend a long section of stairs into the gorge. You'll be following both the Cedar Falls Trail and the 1,400-mile statewide Buckeye Trail. From here you'll follow the blue blazes upstream along Queer Creek to Cedar Falls and back out of the gorge. In the meantime, there's so much scenery it's almost overwhelming: Queer Creek, sandstone cliffs, hemlock forest, spring wildflowers . . . the list goes on. Plan to take your time.

In late winter and early spring, when there is a combination of high water flow and leafless deciduous trees, Hidden Falls will come into view. As you approach (and hear) Cedar Falls, with a green footbridge within sight, look across Queer Creek to your right and up a side drainage. Behind the rocks is Hidden Falls. As you leave Cedar Falls to take steps out of the gorge, you can again look to your right and see Hidden Falls from above.

The loop trail to Cedar Falls is just 0.6 mile. If you're looking to add mileage, follow the BT downstream along Queer Creek for as long as you like before turning around to return to Cedar Falls. During late winter and early spring, high water flow

Cedar Falls, Hocking Hills State Park

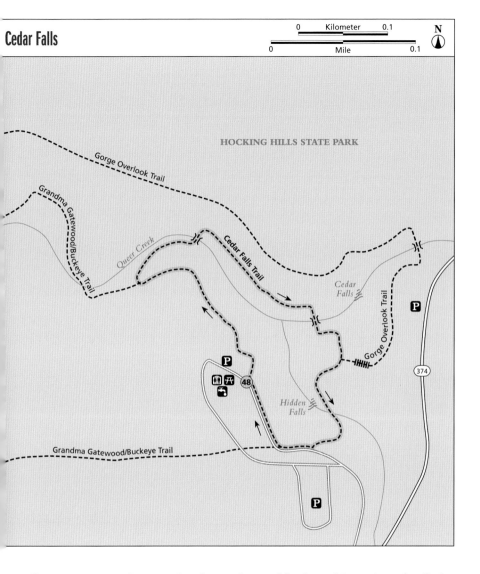

Kilometer 0.1
Mile 0.1

HOCKING HILLS STATE PARK

Gorge Overlook Trail

Grandma Gatewood/Buckeye Trail

Queer Creek

Cedar Falls Trail

Cedar Falls

Gorge Overlook Trail

48

Hidden Falls

374

Grandma Gatewood/Buckeye Trail

will create a series of unnamed, ephemeral waterfalls along this section of trail plus one named waterfall, Whispering Falls. You can walk behind this waterfall where the trail follows a section of boardwalk between the cliff and the falls. Alternatively, you can follow the BT south toward the Hocking State Forest fire tower and then Ash Cave, which is 2.8 trail miles away.

Planning ahead is a good idea when visiting Cedar Falls. This is an extremely popular destination, so if you want to get a photo without a stranger photobombing it, plan to go on a weekday—the earlier the better. Please do not hike off-trail or try to swim in the pool that Cedar Falls plunges into; this is bad for the environment, including flora and fauna, and it prevents others from photographing the falls without you in the photo. (**Note:** When you tag your photos, know that the evergreen trees

Hidden Falls

surrounding the falls are hemlocks. European settlers misnamed this feature Cedar Falls, mixing up the two evergreen species.)

Miles and Directions

0.0 Start at the trailhead kiosk on the north side of the second Cedar Falls parking lot, the one farther from the road. Descend stairs into the gorge on the Cedar Falls Trail.

0.1 Come to a marked junction. Continue straight and cross over a footbridge; the trail then turns right.

0.3 Cross over the creek again on a footbridge and arrive at Cedar Falls just upstream. After checking out the falls, turn back toward the footbridge, but take a left and ascend the stairs out of the gorge. The stairs fork. Continue straight, between the water and the rock face, following the blue blazes.

0.6 The trail comes to the road and parking. Take the trail right as it parallels the road to arrive back at the second parking lot and the trailhead.

Hike Information

Local information: Hocking Hills Tourism Association; (800) HOCKING (800-462-5464), (740) 385-9706; explorehockinghills.com
Organizations: Friends of Hocking Hills State Park; (877) 403-4477
Buckeye Trail Association; (740) 394-2008; buckeyetrail.org
Camping: Hocking Hills State Park Campground; (866) 644-6727; ohiodnr.gov/go-and-do/plan-a-visit/find-a-property/hocking-hills-state-park-campground
Lodging: Hocking Hills State Park Lodge; (800) AT-A-PARK (800-282-7275); ohiodnr.gov/go-and-do/plan-a-visit/find-a-property/hocking-hills-lodge-conference-center

49 Ash Cave Falls

One of the tallest and most beautifully situated waterfalls in Ohio, Ash Cave and its falls would be a major attraction anywhere in the world. Ash Cave is roughly 700 feet wide, 100 feet deep, and 90 feet tall. It's surrounded by old-growth hemlock trees, and the waterfall is the centerpiece. This outing can accommodate people of all interests and abilities: The trail to the cave is paved and wheelchair accessible but then continues in either direction for more than 1,400 miles as part of the statewide Buckeye Trail.

Height of falls: 90 feet
Type of falls: Cave
Distance: 0.6-mile loop
Difficulty: Easy
Hiking time: About 20 minutes
Trail names: Ash Gorge Trail/Buckeye Trail, Ash Rim Trail
Trail surface: Pavement, dirt

Seasons and hours: Good year-round following a rain; open daily, half hour before sunrise to half hour after sunset
Canine compatibility: Dogs permitted on a 6-foot leash
Trailhead facilities: Water, restrooms, picnic area
Trail contact: Hocking Hills State Park; (740) 385-6842; ohiodnr.gov/go-and-do/plan-a-visit/find-a-property/hocking-hills-state-park

Finding the trailhead: From US 33 in Logan, turn south onto SR 664 and go 8.2 miles to SR 374. Turn left (south) and drive 3.7 miles to SR 56. Turn right and go 0.3 mile to the trailhead parking on the right. Additional parking is on the left, across the road. GPS: N39 23.46' / W82 32.43'

The Hike

Ash Cave exemplifies everything the Hocking Hills region is known for: waterfalls, recess caves, gorges. This is the largest recess cave in the Hocking Hills and one of the tallest waterfalls. For these reasons, it's an extremely popular hike, so expect crowds.

Start by walking the paved, wheelchair-accessible Ash Gorge Trail, which is also the Buckeye Trail. Look for the BT's signature blue blazes while you parallel the unnamed run upstream. You are immediately hiking in a gorge, where close-in ridges rise above you on either side. Spring wildflowers here include spring beauty, trillium, foamflower, and many more. Listen and look for a wide variety of birds, from warblers to great blue herons to barred owls. Hemlock trees, which appear along most waterfall hikes in the state, take on new proportions here, with towering old-growth hemlocks surrounding Ash Cave.

Approach and then explore Ash Cave, which measures 700 feet wide, 100 feet deep, and 90 feet tall. It's named for the mounds of ashes that European settlers found when seeing Ash Cave for the first time. This cave sheltered the native Shawnee people for an untold amount of time.

Ash Cave Falls

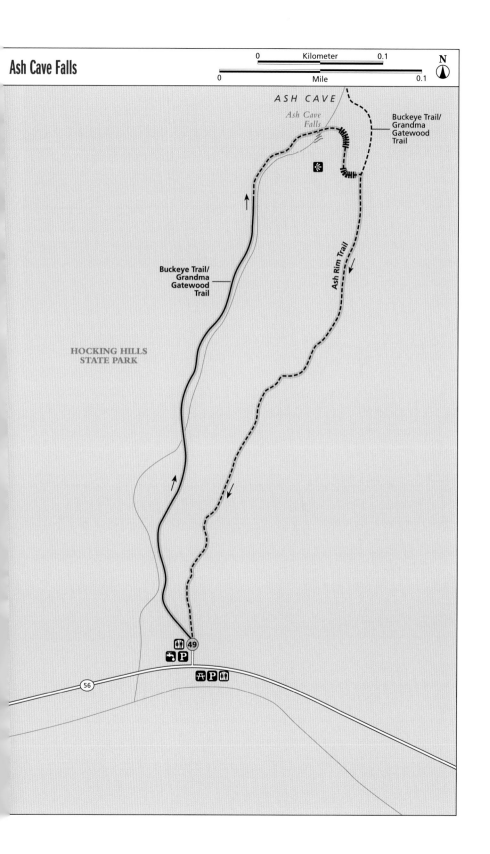

Ash Cave Falls

ASH CAVE

Ash Cave
Falls

Buckeye Trail/
Grandma
Gatewood
Trail

Buckeye Trail/
Grandma
Gatewood
Trail

Ash Rim Trail

HOCKING HILLS
STATE PARK

49

56

Ash Cave Falls

If you or someone in your party needs an ADA-accessible trail, turn back and return the way you came. Otherwise, the trail continues by passing through the rear of the cave, taking you behind the waterfall. The hike itself is a loop, returning on the dirt Ash Rim Trail on the other side of the run, marked with red blazes.

If you want to visit Ash Cave Falls but are looking for a longer hike, no problem. Continue upstream on the Buckeye Trail another 2.8 miles to Cedar Falls, passing a fire tower (that you can climb) halfway in between. Round-trip, that hike is 6.2 miles. Round-trip on the BT from Ash Cave to Upper Falls and back is 13 miles.

Miles and Directions

0.0 Start at the trailhead on the north side of SR 56. Follow the paved path upstream. The Ash Gorge Trail is part of the Buckeye Trail here, marked with blue blazes.

0.2 The paved path ends at Ash Cave. Continue walking through the recess cave. (**Option:** Return directly from here if you need an ADA-accessible trail.)

0.3 Exit the cave by way of wooden stairs. At the top of the stairs, turn right onto the Ash Rim Trail, marked with red blazes.

0.6 Arrive back at the trailhead.

Hike Information

Local information: Hocking Hills Tourism Association; (800) HOCKING (800-462-5464), (740) 385-9706; explorehockinghills.com

Organizations: Friends of Hocking Hills State Park; (877) 403-4477

Buckeye Trail Association; (740) 394-2008; buckeyetrail.org

Camping: Hocking Hills State Park Campground; (866) 644-6727; ohiodnr.gov/go-and-do/plan-a-visit/find-a-property/hocking-hills-state-park-campground

Lodging: Hocking Hills State Park Lodge; (800) AT-A-PARK (800-282-7275); ohiodnr.gov/go-and-do/plan-a-visit/find-a-property/hocking-hills-lodge-conference-center

50 Falls Run Falls

At Boord State Nature Preserve, come for the remoteness and seclusion, and stay for the waterfall. Plan to come in winter or spring to ensure a good flow, as this waterfall can become a trickle in the summer and fall. Spring also brings many flowers, including the state-threatened rock skullcap and golden-knee.

Height of falls: About 15 feet
Type of falls: Tiered, ephemeral
Distance: 0.75-mile loop
Difficulty: Easy
Hiking time: About 20 minutes
Trail name: Boord Trail
Trail surface: Dirt

Seasons and hours: Best in spring; open daily, half hour before sunrise to half hour after sunset
Canine compatibility: Dogs not permitted
Trailhead facilities: None
Trail contact: Boord State Nature Preserve; (740) 380-8919; ohiodnr.gov/go-and-do/ plan-a-visit/find-a-property/boord-state -nature-preserve

Finding the trailhead: From SR 550 halfway between Athens and Marietta, turn south onto CR 6 and go 0.6 mile. Then take a right onto Falls Run Road/TR 69 and go 0.3 mile to the parking pullout on the left. GPS: 39 23.41' / 81 44.48'

The Hike

Like most state nature preserves in Ohio, Boord State Nature Preserve was set aside to help preserve special species—in this case, flora that include the state-threatened rock skullcap (blooming in summer) and golden-knee (late spring through early fall but, sorry, not visible from the trail). Spring is the best time to come, combining more water flow—the waterfall can dry up in summer and fall—with outstanding wildflowers. Also look for Canada mayflower, showy orchids, and white baneberry blooming in the spring. Be sure to stay on the trail, and do not pick any wildflowers.

The hike begins by paralleling Falls Run, which cuts through a hemlock ravine. Once you've hiked to enough waterfalls in Ohio, you'll learn that hemlocks love these cool, wet valleys. Boord is no exception. Very soon you'll come upon a viewing platform for the waterfall below. Think of this short section as a mini Hocking Hills without the crowds. As you continue hiking the counterclockwise loop, exit the ravine and walk through a deciduous forest and then a white pine plantation.

This destination is both remote and primitive. There are no facilities on-site or nearby—no water, no toilet, no picnic table. Plan accordingly. As long as you've come this far, consider visiting a couple of other nearby state nature preserves. Acadia Cliffs is open to visitors without a permit; Ladd Natural Bridge State Nature Preserve requires a permit to visit. Visit the Division of Natural Areas and Preserves website for information about how to get a free permit.

Falls Run Falls

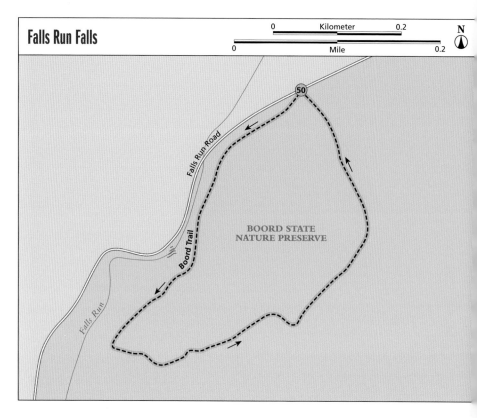

Falls Run Falls

BOORD STATE
NATURE PRESERVE

Miles and Directions

0.0 Start at the trailhead kiosk in the parking pullout. Walk south, paralleling the road.

0.2 Come to the waterfall viewing platform on the right.

0.75 Complete the loop and arrive back at the trailhead where you began.

Hike Information

Local information: Marietta–Washington County Convention & Visitors Bureau; (740) 373-5178; mariettaohio.org

Honorable Mentions

Southeast Ohio

E Ophir Falls

Very close to Lake Katharine State Nature Preserve (hike 41), Coalton Wildlife Area is home to a substantial off-trail waterfall—Ophir Falls. Additionally, there are smaller waterfalls in the wildlife area. This region was once home to the Ophir Iron Company, and this site was once home to the now-defunct Ophir Falls Boy Scout Camp. Because the wildlife area is set aside for hunting and trapping, not hiking, no formal hiking trails exist. Also to that effect: Be sure to wear hunter-orange clothing if you go, as you will be sharing the land with hunters during hunting seasons. To find the falls, you must have very confident off-trail hiking skills and topo map-reading skills. From the parking pullout, you'll take an old logging road more than a mile all the way down to the falls, except for a section of private property, marked with boundary signs. Skirt this section to the west and then return to the old logging road, which joins the stream. Parallel the stream until you arrive at the top of the roughly 20-foot waterfall, quite substantial after a rain. It is a wildlife area, so expect to encounter wildlife, including white-tailed deer and plenty of birds, like woodpeckers, wrens, and cardinals. Spring is the best time to go for water flow, but know that creek crossings can be treacherous then. Spring wildflowers are outstanding, though, and include trillium, jack-in-the-pulpit, Jacob's ladder, and many more.

Trail contact: Coalton Wildlife Area; (740) 589-9930; ohiodnr.gov/go-and-do/plan-a-visit/find-a-property/coalton-wildlife-area

Finding the trailhead: From Coalton, turn west onto Church Street, which becomes Buffalo Skull Road, for 1.8 miles. Once you enter the wildlife area, the road forks. Take the left (west) fork and go 0.1 mile to a small pullout on the right. At the pullout, there is a small meadowy area. Step into this area and look left (south) to find the old logging road. GPS: N39 6.44' / W82 38.29'

White's Mill Falls

F White's Mill Falls

Ohio University was founded in 1804 along the banks of the Hocking River, but classes didn't begin until 1808, with one building, one professor, and three students. A year later, Joseph Herrold built a mill just upstream from campus—along a natural drop in the river, where all the old mills were built. In 1812 the White family bought the mill, and it has been called White's Mill ever since. The original mill burned to the ground in 1913; the building that stands here today is a reconstructed mill from a neighboring county. Somewhere along the line, a dam was built and then later washed out. Today there is no waterwheel, and White's Mill is a garden supply center. Inside, the original grinding stone and roller mill are on display. You can see the concrete and rebar remnants of the old dam. The small waterfall that exists here is a combination of a natural waterfall and dam remnants. Park at the Athens Community Center (mile marker 0) and walk the paved bike path—the Hockhocking Adena Bikeway—all the way to a renovated and relocated little old red schoolhouse between mile markers 3.5 and 4, where you'll get a great view of White's Mill Falls. In between, parallel the Hocking River while skirting the Ohio University campus. At the end of the route, you can follow fishing access trails down to the river. Add in a couple of breweries within walking distance (Jackie O's and Little Fish), and this is a unique waterfalling experience in the state.

Trail contact: Visit Athens County—Athens County Convention & Visitors Bureau; (740) 592-1819; bikeathensohio.com/the-bikeway

Finding the trailhead: From US 33 in Athens, take exit 196 for East State Street. Turn east and go 0.4 mile to the Athens Community Center on the right. From the east end of the parking lot with solar panels, a spur trail takes you to mile 0 on the bike path. GPS: N39 20.10' / W82 4.25'

Hike Index

About the Author

Mary Reed is a freelance writer and photographer based in Athens, Ohio. Her other FalconGuides include *Hiking Ohio, Hiking West Virginia*, and *Best Easy Day Hikes Fort Collins*. Her work has appeared in *Backpacker, Ohio Magazine, Ohio Today*, the *Public Lands Field Guide*, and more. Her favorite place to hike in Ohio is Conkles Hollow State Nature Preserve in the Hocking Hills. You can follow her on Instagram @ maryreehikes or learn more at maryreed.biz.

THE TEN ESSENTIALS OF HIKING

American Hiking Society

American Hiking Society recommends you pack the "Ten Essentials" every time you head out for a hike. Whether you plan to be gone for a couple of hours or several months, make sure to pack these items. Become familiar with these items and know how to use them. Learn more at **AmericanHiking.org/hiking-resources.**

 1. **Appropriate Footwear**

 6. **Safety Items** (light, fire, and a whistle)

 2. **Navigation**

 7. **First Aid Kit**

 3. **Water** (and a way to purify it)

 8. **Knife or Multi-Tool**

 4. **Food**

 9. **Sun Protection**

 5. **Rain Gear & Dry-Fast Layers**

 10. **Shelter**